Powerful an
types and sh,
Jezebel. Bree
untold millic ____ ___ __ ... the business of
spreading the gospel.

Mike Bickle
Founder and Director
International House of Prayer (IHOP), Kansas City

I recommend this book to the true warriors of God to prepare them
for the battle ahead. Dr. Bree Keyton has stepped into a spiritual
realm where many believers are reluctant to journey. The urgency
for God's army to arise is shown in the revelations God has given
her for this book.

Dr. Zalmer J. Nichols,
Th.D., Ph.D., S.Ph.D.
Dean of Faith Bible College

This book is like the cover being pulled off a world of darkness.
Not until this book did we understand what took place several
years ago in our own ministry. We were not equipped to deal with
it at the time...A true Jezebel spirit came to finish us off. Witches
were sent against us...finances dried up, family members started
acting strange, a terrible sulfur smell filled our home...people
would literally sleep, snoring loudly through the services, and
those who were deeper in the Word became weak with a debili-
tating weariness. Finally, we began to learn about this spirit. What
we do not know can hurt us!

Rev. Loula Williams

This book has helped to change my perspective on spiritual
warfare, greatly! ...Many churches and people of God are being
subjected to Jezebel in their midst! This is a wake up call and an
appeal to flow in the Elijah anointing to combat Jezebel in our
pulpits and our lives! ...We must smash Jezebel under our feet!
...We are called to accountability to either walk in the Elijah spirit
or to accept Jezebel's deception...

Sandra Martinez-Cherry

Bree has identified how to pray in these end times. I remember
being confronted with a Jezebel spirit that tore up our church and
my home. This book has helped me see God's Word more clearly.

Saundra Burnett

The Great End Time Clash

Jezebel

vs.

Elijah

Dr. Bree M. Keyton, TH.D., D.C.E.

BLACK FOREST PRESS
San Diego, California
January, 2003
First Edition,Sixth Printing

The Great End Time Clash

Jezebel

vs.

Elijah

Dr. Bree M. Keyton, TH.D., D.C.E.

PUBLISHED IN THE UNITED STATES OF AMERICA
BY
BLACK FOREST PRESS

Cover artwork created by Dan Shanks

Printed in the United States of America
Library of Congress
Cataloging-in-Publication

ISBN: 978-1-58275-052-1
Copyright © February, 2001 by Dr. Bree M. Keyton, TH.D. , D.C.E.
ALL RIGHTS RESERVED

Dedication

Many thanks to my husband and children for their patience and contributions to this book. The blessings of family are unfathomable and a treasure from my Father in Heaven, for which I rejoice!

Table of Contents

Foreword

This is a book I couldn't put down! I stayed up to read it in its entirety the first night I opened it!

Every Christian who sees their calling as that of an Elijah or John the Baptist, "to prepare the way of the Lord, to make paths straight," needs to read this book. This is a must-read book for intercessors and ministers. It gives practical steps on how to overcome the controlling, manipulative, intimidating Jezebel spirit that is so rampant in the Church and society today.

Bree Keyton takes up where most authors have left off. While some authors help readers identify false prophets and spiritually abusive leadership, Bree equips readers with the spiritual weapons to overcome the strongholds that allow these spirits to operate.

As I read this book I felt I had stumbled upon buried treasure. I kept thinking of the people that I needed to share this book with---people who had been spiritually abused, controlled, shamed and broken. Bree's emphasis on humility, forgiveness and repentance brought assurance that the victory is the Lord's, for He opposes the proud but gives grace to the meek.

As Satan fears the end-time clash, we must recognize that his goal is that of Jezebel's---to destroy the prophets and to rob us of the abundant life that Christ has promised us. Anyone who has had the abundant life sucked out of them needs to read the truth that is in this book. Bree accurately applies Truth and this Truth will set the captives free!

Lory Brown, 17 year Missionary
Youth With A Mission (YWAM)

Introduction

Recently, God has led my husband and I, on our ministry outings, into several consecutive encounters with the spirit of Jezebel, through which He has opened our eyes to the intense hatred this wicked spirit has against the servants of YHWH and the moving of the Holy Spirit. Though in various places, through people with differing positions of authority, occupations and genders, the Jezebel spirit manifested the *same* destructive devices.

These divine appointments have presented a virtual catalog of symptoms and evidence that boggled my mind at first, but afterward I realized God's divine purpose was for me to document the characteristics of these spirits, how they interact with people and analyze the data so that I can pass along this much needed information to all the servants of God. Never have I been so aware of the magnitude and seriousness of the spiritual battle we are all engaged in. We must prepare for war, girt up our loins for spirit to spirit combat, apply the blood of Jesus the Christ (Yahshua the Messiah), and become proactive, standing our ground against the evil one.

The spirit of Elijah has begun to move all across the land. The spirit of Elijah is the forerunner spirit, and his coming was foretold by Jesus. The Elijah/forerunner spirit is the spirit of prophecy which is the testimony of Jesus. Jesus is coming again! His body of believers are arising in the spirit of Elijah to defeat the spirit of Jezebel.

The main focus of this book is to reveal how the spirit of Elijah will defeat Jezebel, and to assist the saints in their quest to identify the insidious Jezebel spirit. This must be done before it has a chance to destroy homes, churches and lives, by exposing this wickedness to the light of day and to the power of God. In sharing some of my own successes and failures in ministry, it is my hope that many will benefit from this book and be built up in the LORD.

It is important to state that we have ALL come short of God's plan for our lives. We have all manifested some of Jezebel's characteristics at one time or another. If you recognize some of Jezebel or Ahab in yourself or others, don't get angry, fearful or allow condemnation or accusation to grip you. Instead, get free. Rejoice that darkness is being exposed. Allow the Holy Spirit to bring godly conviction, followed by deep and sincere repentance.

A woman in my college course who is in leadership said, "I was reading your book and suddenly I recognized myself in what you had written. I was shocked, and immediately began to repent. I'm so glad you wrote this book!" Many captives will be set free through this information as we *all* throw ourselves on the mercy of our God. A final caution: The truth will set you free, but it may make you mad first. Don't direct your anger at people; direct it at the devil. He richly deserves it!

Since there are many gods, I have decided to make frequent use of *our* God's Name, YHWH (pronounced Yahweh). Also, I love to call Jesus by His given Hebrew name, Yahshua (some spell this Yeshua) the Messiah. In the movie "Chariots of Fire," the missionary Eric Lyddle, an Olympic athlete, told his wife when she wanted him to give up running and go with her to China, "God made me fast! When I run I feel His pleasure!" I must tell you that when I speak Jesus' true Hebrew name, Yahshua, I feel His pleasure!

All quotations are *KJV*. Word references are from *Strong's Exhaustive Concordance of the Bible*.

Part One

Jezebel
vs.
Elijah

And Ahab told Jezebel all that Elijah had done and withal how he had slain all the prophets with the sword. Then Jezebel sent a messenger unto Elijah, saying, So let the gods do to me, and more also, if I make not thy life as the life of one of them by to-morrow... *1 Kings 19:1-2*

1
Jezebel VS. Elijah

Radical prophets for desperate times

Elijah was a radical prophet sent to King Ahab during desperate times. He cared nothing for what people thought of him, only what God thought. The hairy, mercurial, in-your-face prophet was God's man of the hour, making a strong fashion statement in his goat skin clothing and leather girdle. Out of nowhere he came and into heaven he disappeared. Because most of Israel had bowed their knees to Baal, Elijah was sent to call the people's hearts back to YHWH, the one true God. Elijah declared that it would not rain in Israel, and it did not rain for three and a half years.

Jezebel's influence

Jezebel, the Zidonian princess, became a wicked queen, rebellious wife and mother who usurped the rulership of Israel, causing all Israel to follow her in worshiping Baal and Ashtoreth, in approximately 800 B.C.E. She was the daughter of Ethbaal (meaning Baal's man or with Baal), king of Zidonia (also rendered Sidon), who had murdered his brother to become king. Jezebel's pagan family worshipped Baal and Ashtoreth, and she introduced this perverse religion to Israel, which up until then had, with some exceptions, only worshipped the one true God, YHWH. She turned the people's hearts away from righteousness by marrying the spineless Ahab, king of the Northern Kingdom, which consisted of ten out of the twelve tribes of Israel.

Jezebel was influential in three kingdoms and the spirit that dwelled in her continues to operate beyond her lifetime. She ruled deceptively from within her ivory palace, controlling and dominating her husband and managing to lead the nation in a thirty year reign of despotism. She was a chalice for demonic, unclean spirits that ruled through her with complete control, utterly possessing her soul (mind, will, emotions, imagination and memory).

Jezebel, the person, is gone, but the spirits that indwelled her are alive, acting out the same scenarios today as they did through the flesh and blood woman called Jezebel. It's really quite simple: Whatever the woman Jezebel did almost three thousand years ago, as chronicled in the scriptures, is exactly what the spirit of Jezebel is doing today. There are thousands of people (some nations) worldwide who are possessed by the Jezebel spirit.

The arch enemy

Jezebel was Elijah's arch enemy. Her malice toward him was boundless and she devoted much time to trying to destroy him and his message. While she continually sought to locate him with her spies, she ferociously eradicated the other prophets of YHWH (all but 100 who were hidden). She was reckless and violent in nature, but outwardly she appeared beautiful, draped in her queenly robes against the backdrop of her ivory palace. Inwardly, she resembled a rattlesnake rodeo. She had four hundred prophets of Ashtoreth who dined at her table and fawned on her, while her weakling husband encouraged all Israel to worship at her feet and follow her in the wicked practices of Baal and Ashtoreth worship.

The contest

No person dared oppose Jezebel except Elijah, for her will was supreme. Then came the big showdown on Mount Carmel. Elijah challenged the Baal prophets to a contest. Whichever deity showed up and burned the sacrifice, all the people would worship that god. It was agreed.

The false prophets tried everything to gain their god's attention, but failed, miserably. Their garments were torn and shredded, their bodies streaming with blood. (Today, young people are sewing razor blades in their clothing, drawing blood as they wildly bash dance for attention, but their god is *still* deaf to their cries. I've even observed teens dancing this way in "Christian" coffee houses.)

Elijah stood back mocking and ridiculing the Baal prophets, inciting them into a frenzy, and further acts of self-mutilation. When it was Elijah's turn, then the fireworks began!

YHWH (God) consumed the soaking wet sacrifice made to Him with mighty fire from heaven, and the people began to worship the one true God.

Idols of the king

Elijah had Baal's prophets dragged down to the river where he slew them all. I'm sure they didn't go willingly, but the false prophets of the king *must* fall, for they are nothing compared to the dunamis power of YHWH, King of the Universe.

Since Baal was worshipped as the weather god, YHWH had proven that He was *all* powerful through the drought Elijah had proclaimed. When Elijah prayed, the rains came back.

You and I are living in the days of Elijah once again. With YHWH, events of the past serve as types and shadows of things to come. Despite the persecution, the false prophets must once again fall and the true prophets must arise!

2

Wag the Dog

Jezebel is ruling and reigning again in the idolatrous hearts of people, and they have traded true worship for sensuous wickedness. Deception is the norm. Is the dog wagging the tail or the tail wagging the dog? It is almost time for the tribulation to begin and for Elijah to come back, yet people seem satisfied with the status-quo, a life that is all vanity, deception and idolatrous self-worship; a lifestyle that falls far short of the glorious plan God has for us. There will certainly be a battle between the true prophets of YHWH and the forces of darkness. Will you be ready, with YHWH on the throne of your heart?

Even Elijah ran in fear at Jezebel's threats. John the Baptist, who had Elijah's anointing, began wavering when Herodias threatened him. We are now living in the days of Elijah, again. The spirit of Jezebel is already running rampant, and the forerunner spirit of Elijah is here to proclaim the Word of the LORD, and to draw the father's hearts back to the children, and the children's hearts to the fathers. *(Malachi 4:6; Luke 1:17)* Many will carry this forerunner spirit in great power and demonstration in these last days.

Walking in the anointing and power of Elijah and John the Baptist is a mantle that can only be placed on an individual by God Himself, but as the Father breathes on His servants, many will be stirred to do great exploits and will rise to their destinies for such a time as this.

3

State of
the Union

How did we get such blatantly corrupt people running the White House and our country? There is a spirit behind them, the principality, Jezebel. Judgment will come on this country because of the wickedness of our elected officials, and the travesties of injustice perpetrated on the sleeping public. *But the people who know their God will do great exploits!* Elijah withstood Jezebel, exposed her sin and won! So can we!

There are some believers reading this book who will take courage. May you be strengthened with might (dunamis) by His Spirit in your inner man *(Ephesians 3:16)*, and be preserved blameless unto the coming of our LORD, Yahshua haMashiach (Jesus the Messiah) *(1 Thessalonians 5:23)*.

When YHWH (the LORD) sends us, He watches over us to protect us. He will feed us in times of trouble as He did Elijah. He will keep us safe from the threats of Jezebel, just as He did Elijah, and He will lift us up to be with Him forever, as He did Elijah.

The effectual fervent prayer of a righteous man availeth MUCH. *(James 5:16)*

How much is MUCH? This word, pollos in Greek, means abundant, largely, great, plenteous, a multitude. Can you put "much" in a box and say only *this* much and no more? We serve a mighty God (YHWH) Who created *all* things. He is certainly able to deliver us out of the hand of the wicked.

Spirit of slumber

Jezebel, on the other hand, desires to destroy you and your family. Jezebel brings sensuous pleasures of the flesh, fills your mind up with the stench of sin and the slime of idolatry, lulling a willing people into a spirit of slumber. Then she cuts off their power.

No one notices the filth of porn anymore, since being plagued with it by the evening news during the Lewinsky case and through the porn passing as entertainment in all aspects of the media. The spirit of slumber brings complacency, apathy and submission to wickedness.

A large church I know of was in revival. It got quenched when the "big tithers" declared that they were *uncomfortable* with revival. The pastor shut it down and went back to *his* old program to accommodate the Jezebels who control the money.

Elijah, on the other hand, caused the people to awaken from their slumber and face their idolatrous foolishness. He acted dramatically to rid them of the deception that had blinded their eyes. He called YHWH's people to repentance. Elijah turned the people's hearts back to the living God.

Because the spirit of Elijah is being loosed all across the land, many are rising up, demonstrating and speaking forth prophetic proclamations by the leading and anointing of the Holy Ghost and fire. Each of us must be willing to declare, "Jezebel has been ruling this church and we're not going to tolerate her wickedness anymore. Rise up and repent!" Who cares if Sister Money-Bags leaves. It's better to have the Spirit of God dwelling amongst us, than a bunch of dead, dry bones and a big, fancy building. We *must* want what Jesus wants: a bride prepared for her husband. The rest is irrelevant!

It's critical to take back our congregations for the glory of God before it's too late! Recently, a congregation in Texas witnessed their pulpit being split in two by the sword of the LORD on a Sunday morning. They, and the congregation, yielded up control of the church to the Holy Spirit, and ***they have been in revival ever since!***

4

Jezebel In Our Pulpits

A few years ago, I encountered the spirit of Jezebel inhabiting the pastor of a large church where I was asked to minister in the two Sunday morning services. I proclaimed the Word of the LORD, and ministered healing and deliverance. Twenty to thirty people stood up and declared they'd received healing at each service.

I went home rejoicing and praising God for His glorious presence. On the following Wednesday I received a letter from one of the pastors who was *enraged* that people had been healed. He made some threats and then stated, "If you're going to bludgeon people with Isaiah 53, the least you can do is balance that teaching with suffering and death."

He'd been operating with a strong religious spirit, preaching fear, doubt and unbelief for many years, and as a consequence no one had been healed for a long time in the Jezebel stronghold he had created. He sent letters to all the other pastors he knew, to try to destroy my credibility and stop our ministry permanently.

I discovered that if you throw a rock into a pack of wolves, the one that yelps is the one you hit. I had hit him right in the heart of his most cherished, vulnerable spot: the fabric of lies, deceptions and wicked *unbelief* he had been teaching. He feared exposure. By dramatically and undeniably demonstrating the truth, the people were ecstatic and many were set free, especially the women who had been crushed down for a decade and a half: Whom the Son sets free, is free indeed.

After reading his threats I hid in my room and cried for three days. To be perfectly honest, I was mad at God for sending me into that situation, and at the same time fearful that I had missed His divine plan for that church. Then the LORD spoke to me and told me to go to a certain congregation in the country. When I arrived I was called forward to minister and great and mighty things were wrought by the hand of YHWH that evening. He is surely a loving and merciful God.

I remembered Paul and the vision he received to go to Macedonia where he was hounded by a woman with a spirit of divination, beaten and thrown in jail. Was Paul out of God's will? Did he miss God by going there? No! Paul was victorious because he sang the praises of God even in his deepest, darkest hour. Jezebel had caused great discouragement in me, but my Father in Heaven gave me tasks to do and encouraged me *through* the persecution. I learned how to rejoice when persecution comes, *and it will come for the Word's sake*.

Two minister friends advised me to respond to the attack launched against me by writing or calling the pastor who was responsible. Instead, I hit my knees and began to cry out to YHWH to right the wrongs. I told Him that it was *His* problem since *He* was the one Who sent me into that nest of vipers. I also told Him that if the ministry He had given me shut down because of the persecution, then He could resurrect it or leave it in that state according to His perfect will.

What the devil meant for evil, YHWH turned around for good. What a valuable lesson when we realize that we do not wrestle with people, but rather with the enemy of our souls. I felt comforted when I gave the problem and the weight of the worry to Him, for He brought solace and peace to my soul. I was looking forward to an early retirement.

> **(For the weapons of our warfare are not carnal, but mighty through God to the pulling down of strongholds;) Casting down imaginations, and every high thing that exalteth itself against the knowledge of God, and bringing into captivity every thought to the obedience of Christ. (*2 Corinthians 10:4-5*)**

It was a relief not to have to correspond with my flesh and blood accuser. My heavenly Father was *on the case*. I simply relaxed. I didn't defend myself or fight to prove my point. My Father dealt with this man in a very firm way. He was exposed by YHWH a few months later for the false teacher, doubter, unbeliever and oppressor that he really was, without me having to lift a finger. He also lost his job. Since I knew he was a *doubter*, I prayed he would become a *believer*.

Dearly beloved, avenge not yourselves, but rather give place unto wrath: for it is written, Vengeance is mine; I will repay, saith the Lord. Therefore if thine enemy hunger, feed him; if he thirst, give him drink: for in so doing thou shalt heap coals of fire on his head. Be not overcome of evil, but overcome evil with good. *(Romans 12:19-21)*

Rise up! Be encouraged! Rejoice! *And again I say, rejoice!* The Spirit of the living God is calling for His end-time army: Those who are willing to stand! You cannot operate in *both* fear and faith. You must choose whom you will serve! Learn *now* to operate more and more in faith. Faith will move the hand of God.

Know ye not, that to whom ye yield yourselves servants to obey, his servants ye are to whom ye obey. *(Romans 6:16)*

Begin now to declare that in your country, your city, your church, your job and your household, Jezebel will be thrown down and smashed under foot. Prepare for battle! Put on your armor and plead the blood of Jesus the Messiah over yourself, your family and church. Then get on your knees and go to war. This is the season when a mighty army is being called to stand in the gap.

The shofar is sounding, calling us to war. Jezebel, we serve you notice! We cast you out and we declare your power broken in the Name of Yahshua haMashiach, Jesus the Christ.

Part Two

Clash of the Spirits

All scripture is given by inspiration of God, and is profitable for doctrine, for reproof, for correction, for instruction in righteousness: That the man of God may be perfect, thoroughly furnished unto all good works. *2 Timothy 3:16-17*

5

Announcing the Coming King

Using scripture to illustrate the Elijah spirit and the Jezebel spirit, interspersed with explication, it is my hope that the reader will gain a deeper understanding of the conflict between these two spirits, both in ancient Israel and now. Given the abundance of clues the Word provides, we may begin to know what to expect in our present day.

Jezebel has one master plan: *destroy* the works and people of God. Elijah has one master plan: to expose the works of darkness by *saying* and *doing* the will of God. The end-time clash of these two spirits is beginning to heat up, but this is only the tip of the iceberg. The intensity is being turned up to blast furnace proportions so put on your seat belts; the ride will be bumpy.

In the following chapters, we will be looking at an ancient time when there was only one Jezebel and one Elijah. Today, after 2,800 years of exponential growth, we have thousands, perhaps tens of thousands of people worldwide that are controlled by the spirit of Jezebel.

Even though the church is Jezebel's favorite stomping ground, it is hardly even aware that she exists; yet she is alive and well in virtually every place believers gather together to worship YHWH with a humble spirit and a contrite heart. True worship and praise is like a lightning rod in the spirit realm, drawing her evil hoards to the battle for men's minds and hearts.

At the same time that Jezebel is wreaking havoc, an explosion is taking place in the ministry of Elijah all over the earth. Since the prophetic movement of the last few years began in earnest, the forerunner spirit has been released, bringing a strong awakening and unfolding revelation for a great end-time move of YHWH. We must prepare for the soon coming of our King, Yahshua Messiah (Jesus Christ).

Yahshua is coming again! The first time He came, John the Baptist, who had Elijah's spirit, prepared the way. The coming again of our Creator and King requires a suitable forerunner who announces the arrival of the King. Elijah epitomizes the forerunner spirit and we are the people who are called to move in the spirit of Elijah! We too, are to arise with power from above, prophetic voices so filled with His anointing that we can stop the rain, move mountains, and march against the gates of hell, destroying the armies of Satan.

And it came to pass, as if it had been a light thing for him to walk in the sins of Jeroboam the son of Nebat, that he (Ahab) took to wife Jezebel the daughter of Ethbaal king of the Zidonians, and went and served Baal, and worshipped him. (*1 Kings 16:31*)

Ahab's name means "father's brother." His father, Omri, was a very unscrupulous ruler. He was the most wicked king to rule Israel until Ahab, his son, ruled. Like father, like son! Ahab considered the things of God trivial (as did Esau who lost out on the blessing that Jacob took). He ran after the pleasures of the flesh, being carnal, easily seduced and not having a strong mind of his own. Ahab was easy prey for the conniving Jezebel.

And Elijah the Tishbite, who was of the inhabitants of Gilead, said unto Ahab, As the LORD God of Israel liveth, before whom I stand, there shall not be dew nor rain these years, but according to my Word. (*1 Kings 17:1*)

This prophecy was relevant to the Baal worshiping Israelites, since Baal was thought to be the god of weather. In cutting to the core of the matter by stopping the rain, it revealed that YHWH was the true God. Jezebel set a price on Elijah's head and sent out her spies who hunted for him continually, while he hid first by a brook, later in a widow's house in Zarephath during the drought. The scenario that began with this prophecy, culminated at Mount Carmel three and a half years later: Elijah's confrontation with the prophets of Baal. Following the triumph of YHWH and destruction of the false prophets, Elijah prayed seven times for rain and rain returned to Israel.

...Jezebel slew the prophets of the LORD... (*1 Kings 18:13*)

In a fury over the drought, she killed the true prophets of YHWH so that her false prophets could work their wickedness unchallanged. Her prophets may have been appointed, but they certaintly were **not** anointed.

6

The Challenge On Mount Carmel

The issue between YHWH and Baal was centered upon which god had control of the sky and weather. Baal was worshipped as the god who rode on the clouds, a sky deity who understood lightning, and who set his thunder-bolt in the heavens. YHWH proved His effectual capacity as rain-giver, the true power of the heavens. Unfortunately, in the people's minds, the question was not which god to serve, but which was more powerful.

Elijah returns to make a challenge

And it came to pass, when Ahab saw Elijah, that Ahab said unto him, Art thou he that troubleth Israel? And he answered, I have not troubled Israel; but thou, and thy father's house, in that ye have forsaken the commandments of the LORD, and thou hast followed Baalim. (*1 Kings 18:17-18*)

This is the basic deception of Satan. His followers believe that God's prophets are against them, when in fact, YHWH sends the prophets to save them from themselves. Elijah was not troubling Israel. Through him, God was wooing Israel back to Himself.

Now therefore send, and gather to me all Israel unto Mount Carmel, and the prophets of Baal four hundred and fifty, and the prophets of the groves four hundred, which eat at Jezebel's table. (*1 Kings 18:19*)

Eight hundred and fifty false prophets were called to gather against YHWH for the big showdown. When the false prophets were shown to be charlatans, they were destroyed.

> **So Ahab sent unto all the children of Israel, and gathered the prophets together unto Mount Carmel.** *(1 Kings 18:20)*

The people and the prophets were sent for: 450 prophets at Samaria (Baal's prophets) and 400 prophets (Ashtoreth's prophets) that ate at Jezebel's table in Jezreel. Since it was Baal who was being challenged, Ashtoreth's prophets may not have attended. Four hundred prophets appeared later in Ahab's court when Micaiah prophesied, and though it is unclear in scripture, it may have been these same prophets. *(1 Kings 22:6)*

> **And Elijah came unto all the people, and said, How long HALT ye between two opinions? if the LORD be God, follow Him: but if Baal, then follow him. And the people answered him not a word.** *(1 Kings 18:21)*

Elijah called upon the people to choose but they refused to speak. They had gathered to see THE SHOW. Wavering, double-minded men will bend whichever way the wind blows and cannot be counted on to remain steadfast.

HALT means pursuing a vacillating and irregular course. This was reflected in the people's indecision as they wavered between serving YHWH and Baal. Halt became a metaphor for half-hearted, double-minded indecision. Halt also meant "limping." It reflected the peculiar ritual dance the false prophets performed, hopping from one leg to another, as they leaped about (limped about) performing a weird and uncouth dance around the altar. (1)

> **Then said Elijah unto the people, I, even I only, remain a prophet of the LORD; but Baal's prophets are four hundred and fifty men.** *(1 Kings 18:22)*

This is a similar lament to the one Elijah wailed to the LORD after he ran from Jezebel. *(1 Kings 19:14)* He claimed he was the only remaining prophet in Israel.

The second time he made this statement the LORD told him there were seven thousand people who had not bowed their knee to Baal. YHWH always has a remnant. We can take courage from this truth; no matter how bad things get, we are not alone. Our heavenly Father has others who will not yield to Satan.

> **And call ye on the name of your gods, and I will call on the name of the LORD (YHWH): and the God that answereth by fire, let him be God. And all the people answered and said, It is well spoken.** *(1 Kings 18:24)*

The people acted as umpires and sat as a jury. It is to the people that Elijah directed the contest. The God who could focus His lightning precisely on a small altar was worthy to be called God.

> **And it came to pass at noon, that Elijah mocked them, and said, Cry aloud: for he is a god; either he is talking, or he is pursuing, or he is on a journey, or peradventure he sleepeth, and must be awaked.** *(1 Kings 18:27)*

Elijah taunted the prophets of Baal. He mocked their ineffective ritual. One Bible version indicates that Elijah asked them if their god had gone to the toilet!

> **And they cried aloud, and cut themselves after their manner with knives and lancets, till the blood gushed out upon them.** *(1 Kings 18:28)*

The false prophets became frantic and began to scream and cut themselves. Ritual abuse was common. After all, they believed the worship of their god had solar implications and that he had destructive powers. They thought their hysterical blood-letting would draw their "gods" to them by inviting a blood covenant with their deity. They spent six hours trying to illicit their god's attention, blood was gushing, and still no answer.

Leaping around the altar may have also been performed to induce a trance-like state. Cutting themselves was a substitute for human sacrifice. (2) Additionally, blood-letting may have been a rite of imitative magic to promote new life, or bring rain. (3)

7

The God That Answers By Fire

And it came to pass, when midday was past, and they prophesied until the time of the offering of the evening sacrifice, that there was neither voice, nor any to answer, nor any that regarded. *(1 Kings 18:29)*

They "prophesied" falsely, and got no answer. The hour was late. Baal could not produce thunder, or lightening, he had no voice, no clouds. Baal's expertise was shown to be defective.

And Elijah said unto all the people, Come near unto me. And all the people came near unto him. And he repaired the altar of the LORD that was broken down. *(1 Kings 18:30)*

Elijah drew the people near. Contrasting his prayer against the antics of the Baal prophets, he remained quiet, calm and confident.

And Elijah took twelve stones, according to the number of the tribes of the sons of Jacob, unto whom the word of the LORD came, saying Israel shall be thy name: And with the stones he built an altar in the name of the LORD: and he made a trench about the altar... *(1 Kings 18:31-32)*

Elijah repaired the ancient altar of YHWH using twelve stones to point toward unity of the twelve tribes of Israel and the promises of YHWH.

...Fill four barrels with water, and pour it on the burnt sacrifice, and on the wood. And he said, Do it the second time. And they did it the second time. And he

said, Do it the third time. And they did it the third time. And the water ran round about the altar; and he filled the trench also with water. *(1 Kings 18:33-35)*

It was a long way down, 470 feet, to fetch water from the bottom to the top of the mountain. Pouring water signifies repentance and cleansing of sin. Elijah was heightening the drama and suspense of the contest by repeatedly soaking the sacrifice. Notice there were four barrels, filled three times, making twelve barrels of water poured on the sacrifice. This was deliberately done to point symbolically, once again, to the twelve tribes of Israel as a whole unit in YHWH's eyes.

And it came to pass, at the time of the offering of the evening sacrifice, that Elijah the prophet came near and said, LORD God of Abraham, Isaac, and of Israel, let it be known this day that Thou art God in Israel, and that I am Thy servant, and that I have done all these things at Thy Word. *(1 Kings 18:36)*

Evening sacrifice was at about 3 PM. Elijah came near to pray so that the people could hear him. This was reminiscent of Jesus' prayer at Lazarus' tomb in which He prayed out loud for Lazarus to be raised from the dead so that the people could hear him and believe God had sent Him. Elijah, too, desired in his prayer that God would be glorified and his own ministry validated.

Hear me, O LORD, hear me, that this people may know that Thou art the LORD God, and that Thou hast turned their heart back again. *(1 Kings 18:37)*

Elijah prayed out loud to the true God so all heard and saw how YHWH mightily demonstrates His power. He further revealed that YHWH was wooing the people's hearts back to Himself.

Then the fire of the LORD fell, and consumed the burnt sacrifice, and the wood, and the stones, and the dust, and licked up the water that was in the trench. *(1 Kings 18:38)*

God's mighty fire fell, as lightning from a cloudless sky, on the soaking wet wood and sacrifice, and consumed it. This was proof to the Israelites of God's existence and power.

And when all the people saw it they fell on their faces: and they said, The LORD, He is the God; the LORD, He is the God. *(1 Kings 18:39)*

In Hebrew rendering, the people said, "YHWH, He is Elohim." Elijah's demonstration brought the people's hearts back to the true God. Baal's impotence was clearly demonstrated for all to see. This contest had implications far beyond Israel, reaching into every corner of the world.

And Elijah said unto them, Take the prophets of Baal; let not one of them escape. And they took them: and Elijah brought them down to the brook Kishon, and slew them there. *(1 Kings 18:40)*

Elijah slew all the prophets of Baal, personally. This was a picture of what will happen to all who follow Jezebel and her idols, past, present and future.

And Elijah said unto Ahab, Get thee up, eat and drink; for there is a sound of abundance of rain. *(1 Kings 18:41)*

Elijah tries to encourage Ahab. Ahab needed it. He looked to Ahab's natural needs, but the intent is clearly to bring strength to the king for his upcoming battle with Jezebel.

Elijah further proclaimed his faith when he declared there is the *sound* of the abundance of rain. This was the final nail in the coffin of Baal worship. With the Baal prophets dead, YHWH sent rain, proving *He alone* is the supreme God; Baal a useless statue.

8

From the Heights of Triumph To the Depths of Despair

Facing Jezebel is a lesser challenge than Mount Carmel, yet at her vindictive threats, in a state of confusion and exhaustion, Elijah ran for his life. What should have convinced Jezebel and turned her toward the true God, served to further harden her heart.

> ...And Ahab told Jezebel all that Elijah had done, and withal how he had slain all the prophets with the sword. *(1 Kings 19:1)*

Ahab ran to Jezebel like a whipped puppy and told her what happened. This was his big chance to stand up and declare the greatness of YHWH, but he feared Jezebel more than YHWH. She cast a long shadow. Ahab suffered from fear of man. He was under Jezebel's spell. He was her creature, helpless when he should be victorious. The glorious chance for a new beginning for Israel, won by the boldness of Elijah, was lost by the spineless wimp, Ahab.

> Then Jezebel sent a messenger unto Elijah, saying, So let the gods do to me, and more also, if I make not thy life as the life of one of them (slain false prophets) by tomorrow about this time. *(1 Kings 19:2)*

This was an obvious attempt at intimidation, *and it worked.* Jezebel was a bluffer. She threatened when she could have sent troops. She knew the people were behind Elijah at that time, and it was *she* who was in fear. She was enraged at the prophet's bold stand against her and her idols. Her dignity as a queen had been challenged, and her religious sensibilities had been insulted. She sought revenge by setting a price on Elijah's head...again.

> **And when he (Elijah) saw that, he arose, and went (fled) for his life...** *(1 Kings 19:3)*

Her tactics worked for her reputation preceeded her. Elijah, the conquering hero ran away. After great victories, this is the time when Satan often defeats his enemies through fear, discouragement, pride and deception.

> **But he himself (Elijah) went a day's journey into the wilderness, and came and sat down under a juniper tree: and he requested for himself that he might die; and said, It is enough; now, O LORD, take away my life; for I am not better than my fathers.** *(1 Kings 19:4)*

Wow! Could this be the same Elijah, who just two days earlier stood before multitudes mocking Baal's prophets, extolling YHWH's power and slaying His enemies? Now he wanted to die after realizing he was *not* better than his fathers. How quickly we can fall from the pride of life, and fail from the fear of man.

> **...And, behold, the LORD passed by, and a great and strong wind rent the mountains, and brake in pieces the rocks before the LORD; but the LORD was not in the wind: and after the wind an earthquake; but the LORD was not in the earthquake; And after the earthquake a fire; but the LORD was not in the fire: and after the fire a still small voice.** *(1 Kings 19:11-12)*

YHWH was not in the fire, the earthquake, or the whirlwind. He wanted Elijah to see Him as more than just the forces of nature as Baal was viewed, or as a mere tribal deity. YHWH demonstrated that He is omnipresent, omniscient, omnipotent and transcendent. The still, small voice drew Elijah on to a deeper understanding of his God.

> **And the LORD said unto him, Go, return on thy way to the wilderness of Damascus: and when thou comest, anoint Hazael to be king over Syria: And Jehu the son of Nimshi shalt thou anoint to be king over**

Israel: and Elisha the son of Shaphat of Abelmeholah shalt thou anoint to be prophet in thy room. And it shall come to pass, that him that escapeth the sword of Hazael shall Jehu slay: and him that escapeth from the sword of Jehu shall Elisha slay. *(1 Kings 19:15-17)*

The LORD responded to Elijah's pity party by giving him important work to do. He was to anoint two kings, Hazael and Jehu, and begin to groom his own successor. When it seemed to Elijah that the ministry was over, God redeemed the situation.

Yet I have left me seven thousand in Israel, all the knees which have not bowed unto Baal... *(1 Kings 19:18)*

The still, small voice brought comfort, and showed Elijah that he was *not* alone in his service and zeal for YHWH. The seven thousand that had not bowed their knee to Baal were hiding in the mountains and Elijah didn't know about them.

The tasks YHWH called Elijah to at this moment completed the work that began with his entrance on the scene in Israel. Elisha, wearing his mantle, completed Elijah's work. Hazael's men killed Ahab and Jehu killed the sons of Ahab and his wife, Jezebel.

9

Jezebel Gives Ahab
The Vineyard

Jezebel did not see herself as bound by the same constrictions of the law as Ahab. In the despotic background she sprang from, rulers simply took what they wanted. She had no tolerance for the limitations YHWH put on covenant property, while Ahab had no stomach for the kill. Thus, she was much harder to deal with than Ahab. The vineyard was not Jezebel's to give. She usurped authority in a cunning way and seized power from the king.

And it came to pass after these things, that Naboth the Jezreelite had a vineyard, which was in Jezreel, hard by the palace of Ahab king of Samaria. *(1 Kings 21:1)*

Jezreel was the site of Ahab's winter palace. (His main palace was in Samaria.) Naboth's vineyard was right next to the palace.

And Ahab spake unto Naboth, saying, Give me thy vineyard, that I may have it for a garden of herbs, because it is near unto my house... *(1 Kings 21:2)*

A vineyard required many years of time, effort and investment before it matures. Ahab would have destroyed all this for a vegetable garden.

And Naboth said unto Ahab, The LORD forbid it me, that I should give the inheritance of my fathers unto thee. *(1 Kings 21:3)*

The land was not Naboth's to give. A man's inheritance was his father's and his son's.

> And Ahab came into his house heavy and displeased
> because of the word which Naboth the Jezreelite had
> spoken to him: for he had said, I will not give thee the
> inheritance of my fathers. And he laid him down upon
> his bed, and turned away his face, and would eat no
> bread. *(1 Kings 21:4)*

What a pouter! He won't eat because he didn't get his way. It
sounds like a possible regular routine with him, one which Jezebel
was familiar with.

> But Jezebel his wife came to him (Ahab), and said
> unto him, Why is thy spirit so sad, that thou eatest no
> bread? And he said unto her, Because I spake unto
> Naboth the Jezreelite, and said unto him, Give me
> thy vineyard for money...he answered, I will not give
> thee my vineyard. *(1 Kings 21:5-6)*

Naboth was righteous to keep his property. Under the law of
Moses, property belonged to a family forever and was not to be
sold. Ahab's peevish sulking opened the door to Jezebel who had
no scruples. In his heart he knew the justness of Naboth's claim.
He was simply not man enough to accept it.

> And Jezebel his wife said unto him, Dost thou now
> govern the kingdom of Israel? arise, and eat bread, and
> let thine heart be merry: I WILL GIVE THEE THE
> VINEYARD of Naboth the Jezreelite. *(1 Kings 21:7)*

She stated that "she will give him the vineyard." This was
reminiscent of Satan's temptation of Jesus, when he said: All
these things will I give Thee, if Thou wilt fall down and
worship me. *(Matthew 4:9)* Jezebel mocked her husband, then
she easily slid into a position of control. She seduced him by encouraging him to make merry while she did the dirty work *in his
name*, usurping his leadership. He was only too glad to do her
bidding and wash his hands of the difficult task of leading a
nation. If we are not vigilant, Jezebel will usurp our sovereignty,
and send us to destruction, as well.

Jezebel and Ahab openly displayed disdain for God's law.
Jezebel will not play any game she cannot control, nor will
she submit to anyone or live (cohabit) with anyone she cannot

control. The name Jezebel means "without cohabitation." From her heart, she yields to no one. She will lie in wait, lurking in the shadows until the odds are in her favor and then she will execute her devious plot. Meanwhile, she cruises the hallway looking for an open door, where a weak *king or priest* (all believers are kings and priests) will yield to her opportunistic nature. This is how the devil works, watching and waiting for you to drop your guard, and in a moment of weakness he pounces and devours.

10

Jezebel Takes
A Nation
With Idolatry

Jezebel introduces pagan worship

Jezebel introduced the pagan religion of the Phoenicians and Canaanites (who worshipped Bel or Belus, identical god to Baal) to Israel, and Ashtoreth worship. Ashtoreth (Asherah or Astarte) was probably represented by carved wooden poles set up next to statues of Baal. The Canaanites believed that Ashtoreth ruled the sea, was the mother of all the gods including Baal and was the consort of Baal.

Jezebel was a rebellious and manipulative queen. She caused ten million Israelites to follow Baal, while only seven thousand remained faithful to YHWH. She corrupted a whole nation with her idolatry as she relentlessly pursued her efforts to destroy the worship of YHWH. She was determined and savage in her attempt to eradicate YHWH's prophets. Jezebel's father was the high priest of Ashtoreth in Zidonia (4) and she inherited his passion for the cruel pagan worship of Baal and Ashtoreth.

At an excavation at Megiddo, in the ruins of a temple of Ashtoreth at Gezer, where the Canaanite's worshipped Baal and Ashtoreth, there were found great numbers of jars containing remains of sacrificed newborn babies. The prophets of Baal and Ashtoreth were murderers of children. The people also engaged in another practice called "foundation sacrifice." It was thought to be good luck to sacrifice an infant and build its body into the wall of new structures. (5)

Enormous quantities of images and plaques of Ashtoreth were found with exaggerated sex organs, designed to foster sensual feelings. Temples of Baal and Ashtoreth were built together. The enclosures were 150 X 120 feet surrounded by a wall open to the sky. Ten stone pillars, five to eleven feet high were placed where sacrifices were offered.

Worship was conducted in groves of trees which were cultivated and allowed to grow right in the temples. Trees were also worshipped. Pliny, the historian, reveals that trees were the first temples, and afterward temples were built among the trees. (6)

King Ahab formally adopted Jezebel's religion (7) and the people were willing and eager to receive it because their foolish hearts were darkened through rebellion against the true God of Israel. Ahab's greatest crime was marrying Jezebel. Under her seduction he was demonically inspired to promote and support paganism.

> **And it came to pass, as if it had been a light thing...that he (Ahab) took to wife Jezebel...and went and served Baal, and worshiped him...and Ahab did more to provoke the LORD God of Israel to anger than all the kings of Israel that were before him.** *(1 Kings 16:31-33)*

Ahab built two temples to Baal and Ashtoreth. In the ruins of Ahab's palace were found Jezebel's small stone box and saucers in which she mixed her cosmetics, green, red and black. Some red was still in one of them, (8) perhaps left on the day she hurried to adorn herself seductively for Jehu's arrival.

Jezebel is the seed of Baal

Jezebel's father's name was Ethbaal, meaning Baal's man. The seed of God rose to destroy the seed of Baal. The story of Jezebel versus Elijah is of eternal significance. It is a story of good vs. evil: The forces of God against the forces of darkness. God always triumphs! God was merciful over and over in Ahab and Jezebel's lives, yet they turned their backs on Him to play the harlot with Baal.

> **...He will thoroughly purge His floor, and gather His wheat into the garner; but He will burn up the chaff with unquenchable fire.** *(Matthew 3:12)*

That was then and this is now

Our God retained a faithful remnant then, and He has a faithful remnant now! The temptation to serve false gods is just as real today as it was in the time of King Ahab. As the spirit of Jezebel arises, so will the spirit of Elijah.

> **Now the Spirit speaketh expressly, that in the latter times some shall depart from the faith, giving heed to seducing spirits, and doctrines of devils; Speaking lies in hypocrisy; having their conscience seared with a hot iron...** *(1 Timothy 4:1-2)*

> **...in the last days perilous times shall come. For men shall be lovers of their own selves, covetous, boasters, proud, blasphemers, disobedient to parents, un-thankful, unholy, without natural affection, truce breakers, false accusers, incontinent (no self-control), fierce, despisers of those that are good...lovers of pleasures more than lovers of God...** *(2 Timothy 3:1-4)*

We may not call the sins committed today Baal worship, but people indulge in the same reckless wickedness as they did in Jezebel's day. The above scriptures sound as if they were taken right out of today's headlines, not written two thousand years ago.

11

Origins of Baal and Ashtoreth

Baal (meaning possessor, sun or lord) was a male deity of fertility and weather, whose divine powers were limited to nature. He was the fertility cult's most active deity. Known as the sun god and the storm god, he was expressed as a helmeted warrior in short kilt, striding into action with a thunderbolt as a spear, mace uplifted. The bull was his cult animal, and horns were worn on his helmet. Baal was known as a dying and risen god, signified by the rising and setting sun, and as having victory over Chaos. (9) He was worshipped with sacrifices, both human and animal, by burning incense and burnt offerings (especially bullocks), and by kissing his image. (10)

Ashtoreth was the corresponding female deity, simultaneously worshipped. She was known as the goddess of love, sexual immorality, and the giver of life and death. She was the patron goddess of fertility. Temples of pleasure and legalized vice were built as worship to this goddess and proliferated throughout Israel. She was believed to be the authoress of sexual passion and helper of men, freeing them from sickness and the curse of sin and guilt. (11) In other words, through her, people could *do anything they liked*, and taught to believe they were not being held accountable for their sins. No wonder everyone wanted to worship these gods.

Worship of self

In essence, the worship of Baal and Ashtoreth was the religion of self-worship, self will, lewd, indulgent, reckless behavior, acted out in sodomy, sex orgies and perversion. Priestesses were actually temple prostitutes. Sodomites were made male temple prostitutes. They had extravagant orgies when worshiping their gods. (12)

The priests of Baal danced with frantic shouts around the altar, and cut themselves with knives to excite attention from their god. Ashtoreth was deified through sensuousness and legitimized sexual indulgence. Prayers or vows were made with magic rituals to influence these deities through the priests auto-suggestions. (13)

Origin of pagan religions

Cush, eldest of the sons of Ham (who was Noah's youngest son) was known to ancient pagans as Bel, the Confounder. The ancients called him Chaos. He was known as the god of confusion because he founded Babylon. Other names for Cush are Mercury and Hermes (meaning son of Ham). He was the original prophet of idolatry and the ringleader of the great apostasy. (14) Under his leadership all language was confounded and the people were scattered. His wife was the infamous Semiramis.

Cush's son, Nimrod or Ninus (meaning son), was an ambitious, warlike man, who built the great Babylon and other cities. He is renowned for subduing the horse for the chase and taming the leopard (may have been cheetahs) for hunting other beasts. "Nimr" meaning a leopard, and "rada or rad" meaning to subdue, form the name Nimrod, meaning "to subdue leopards." (15)

> **And Cush begat Nimrod: he began to be a mighty one in the earth: He was a mighty hunter BEFORE the LORD: wherefore it is said, Even as Nimrod the mighty hunter BEFORE the LORD. And the beginning of his kingdom was Babel...** (*Genesis 10:8-10*)

The word BEFORE actually means AGAINST the LORD. Nimrod was rebellious and ripe for judgment. What his father began, he promoted with a vengeance. He was the first man to conduct war with his neighbors.

Semiramis was both Nimrod's mother and his wife. In Egypt Semiramis and Nimrod were known as Isis and Osiris, a mother and son. He bore as one of his titles the name "Husband of the Mother." Together they were worshipped throughout the known world. Nimrod (historically also known as Ninus) is additionally known as *Tammuz*. (16)

The women ritually "wept for forty days for Tammuz" beginning soon after he was torn to pieces (legendarily, but not

actually, by a wild boar). Thus, for the purpose of revenge and re-
membrance, we have the origins of killing a pig and eating ham on
Easter. The forty days of abstinence and sorrow know as lent are
directly borrowed from worship of the Babylonian god, Tammuz,
preceding the pagan holiday celebration of the birth of the pagan
fertility goddess, Easter (another name for Semiramis). This
ancient pagan festival alternates between weeping and rejoicing
for the death and resurrection of Tammuz. (17)

Easter is not a Christian name. Its Chaldean origin is Astarte
meaning Queen of Heaven. The Assyrians knew the name as
Ishtar. This holiday was celebrated at about the same time as the
Jewish Passover. The egg, used as a symbol for Easter, has
heathen roots. The mystic egg of Astarte, was adopted by the
Roman Church as a *symbol* of Christ's resurrection along with
many other pagan rituals during Constintine's reign. According to
legend, a large egg fell from heaven into the Euphrates River, fish
rolled it to the bank where doves hatched it, and out came
Venus, the Syrian goddess (Astarte, Semiramis). The egg, additionally, was tied mysteriously to the origin of the world, which
according to legend was shut up in an egg floating on the waters,
represented the ark floating on the waters containing Noah's
family. (18)

> **Then   he brought me (Ezekiel) to the door of the
> gate of the LORD's house which was toward the
> north; and, behold, there sat women WEEPING FOR
> TAMMUZ...And he brought me into the inner court
> of the LORD's house, and, behold, at the door of the
> temple of the LORD, between the porch and the altar,
> were about five and twenty men, with their backs
> toward the temple of the LORD, and their faces toward
> the east; and they worshipped the sun toward the
> east. (*Ezekiel 8:14-16*)**

This weeping was an abomination against YHWH and became
known in later centuries as Lent, a forty day time of purification,
weeping and fasting. [The weeping in Greece where Bacchus
(or Bakhah), another name for Tammuz, was worshipped proliferated and was adopted by the Roman Church when they set out to
blend pagan religions with Christianity. (19) The name Bacchus
means *weeping* or "the lamented one."] Notice the men were
worshiping toward the east, where the sun comes up, for the god

they worshipped was the "sun god." Sunrise services on Easter
Sunday are really a throwback to ancient pagan rituals that were
common for the rising of the sun god. (20) The switching of
worship from the Sabbath, sundown Friday to sundown Saturday,
over to Sunday (sun god day), is further proof of the paganization
of Christianity. Incidentally, December 25 is the actual birthday of
Tammuz. Jesus (Yahshua) was born in the fall when it was still
warm enough for shepherds to be in the field. His probable birth
date, according to the calculations of Michael James Rood, was on
the Feast of Tabernacles, the day God came to dwell with men.

A generational curse was on Nimrod that began with the sin of
Ham, his grandfather, youngest son of Noah. Ham's forth son was
Canaan and the land named after him became known as a place
where idolatry and sin abounded. *(Genesis 9:18)* Canaan received
the curse for Ham's indecency toward his father, Noah.

**And Noah awoke from his wine, and knew what his
younger son had DONE unto him. And he said,
Cursed be Canaan: a servant of servants shall he be
unto his brethren. And he said, Blessed be the LORD
God of Shem; and Canaan shall be his servant.**
(Genesis 9:24-26)

Jewish oral tradition indicates that Ham's sin against his father
was of a homosexual nature. The hurt of the subsequent rejection
by his father fostered rebellion in Ham which increased exponentially through at least two of his sons, Cush and Canaan, and his
grandson, Nimrod (Tammuz). *(Genesis 9:22, 25)*

Zidon was the firstborn of Canaan, Ham's son, who founded
the city of Zidon (also Sidon). It is through this cursed bloodline
that Jezebel ultimately was born. Because of his idolatry,
Nimrod was killed by Shem (eldest son of Noah who had received
Noah's special blessings). Nimrod's body was chopped up into
twelve pieces and sent to all parts of the kingdom as a warning
against practicing pagan worship. (21)

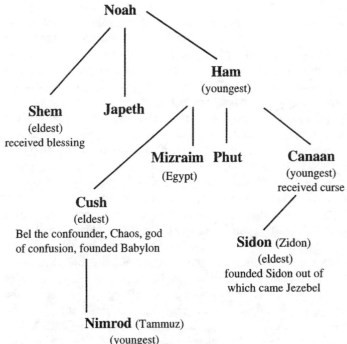

Noah

Shem
(eldest)
received blessing

Japeth

Ham
(youngest)

Mizraim Phut
(Egypt)

Canaan
(youngest)
received curse

Cush
(eldest)
Bel the confounder, Chaos, god
of confusion, founded Babylon

Sidon (Zidon)
(eldest)
founded Sidon out of
which came Jezebel

Nimrod (Tammuz)
(youngest)
subdued leopards, first to declare war, mighty
hunter "against" the LORD, founded Ninevah,
built Babylon, married his own mother

Jezebel's precursor: Semiramis

Semiramis was compelled to go underground after this gory incident with her new religion (thus mystery Babylon). The mystery religions, including Masonry, were born out of Semiramis' need for secrecy. She proceeded to deify her son as the "sun god," making herself the "moon goddess."

There were many names given to Nimrod as the worship of pagan deities spread throughout the kindreds, tribes and nations of the world. Here are a few: [Adonis, Apollo, Atlas, Bacchus, Bel, Beelzebub, Molech, Dionysus, Hermes, Mercury, Kronos, Saturn, Osiris, Amun-re (also, Amen Ra and Ra), Orion, Phaethon, Mars, Siva, Tammuz, Vulcan, Narcissus, Linus, Memnon, Kamut, Zeus, Juno, Odin, Wodan, Thor, Jupiter, etc.].

The first deified woman, Semiramis, also had many names among peoples and nations: [Easter, Ishtar, Diana, Europa (for which the continent of Europe was named), Venus, Ceres, Minerva,

Lakshmi, Kali, Ariadne, Aphrodite, Astarte, Ashtoreth, Queen of Heaven (still worshipped by Catholics), Rhea, Aurora, Isis, etc.].

Ashtoreth was often more highly revered than Baal. This is not surprising, considering how worship of these two deities began. The mother, Semiramis, upon the violent death of her son and husband, Nimrod, had all the pieces of his body recovered and returned, except one, which was lost. (22)

To symbolize the lost part, she had giant phallic symbols built at Nimrod's altars. Down through the centuries these steeples continued. Placed originally by his altars, they were later placed on roofs to let everyone know where "sun worship" was taking place. Horns of a bull, which he had won and worn in life, symbolic of his great ability as a hunter, was another symbol of Nimrod worship.(23) Thus, Baal was invented, the horned bull-god of Babylon. Satan, himself, is often symbolized as a horned-bull deity.

After death, Nimrod was worshipped as the "sun god." His mother was worshipped as the "mother of god," and the "moon goddess." They were often depicted as a madonna and child, with a nimbus (halo) around their heads, signifying sun worship, or the shining of the sun, thus completing their self-portrayal as gods. (24)

The depiction of Jesus and His mother Mary with halo's around their heads, in millennia later art, is actually a carry over from ancient pagan depictions of Semiramis and Tammuz. Notice in these paintings that the artist always shows the Madonna as an adult, and her son as a babe in her arms. This, too, came from Semiramis, who, as establisher of their religion often had preeminence over her son in pagan worship. This is still true in some religions where the mother of the son of god is worshipped and more highly exalted than the son himself. Some religions pray to the mother and beg her to intercede for them to their god. The Queen of Heaven, originally Semiramis, is known as the mediatrix of all graces. Pagan worshippers believe she interceedes between god and man.

Worshiping and praying to the Queen of Heaven is an abomination to Jesus, who is our sole mediator.

For there is one God, and one mediator between God and men, the man Christ Jesus; Who gave Himself a ransom for all... (*1 Timothy 2:5-6*)

...He is the   mediator of the new testament, that by means of death, for the redemption of the transgressions...they...might receive...eternal inheritance. (*Hebrews 9:15*)

12

Jezebel Desires To Possess God's Vineyard

Jezebel unmasked

Jezebel's true character is that of a despot, a deceiver, a backstabber, a usurper, a murderer, a great whore and promoter of false religion, a pervert, a controller, a people user, etc. She accomplishes her goals clandestinely under the guise and name of another, while hiding behind true power. She commits acts of deception in order to disguise her true agenda. She kills (discredits, destroys) the true prophets and installs her own false prophets in order to take over a country, property, a congregation, a home, a business, etc.

> So she wrote letters IN AHAB'S NAME, and sealed them with his seal, and sent the letters unto the elders and to the nobles that were in his city, dwelling with Naboth. And she wrote in the letters, saying, Proclaim a fast, and set Naboth on high among the people: and set two men, sons of Belial, before him, to bear witness against him...and stone him, that he may die. *(1 Kings 21:8-10)*

She used deceit to destroy many. She used another's name to gain control, but it should be noted that she probably had, at the very least, Ahab's tacit approval, if not full collusion. She took advantage of a solemn fast and confession time to execute her plan. Two witnesses were required by law. Enough adult males would be present at the fast to constitute a judicial quorum. She plotted and schemed destruction for the innocent Naboth, so that what Ahab could not buy, he could now take.

Naboth, in his innocence, becomes a type of Jesus. He is falsely accused as Jesus was falsely accused. This occurs during a sacred ceremony; Jesus' trial was during Passover. Leaders of the nation plotted to destroy him as they did Jesus and Naboth's sons were pursued and destroyed as many followers (sons of God) of Jesus were martyred for their faith. The enemy, Jezebel, wished to take the vineyard as the devil wishes to take the vineyard of humanity away from Jesus.

Jezebel's power play

Ahab pouted and whined like a peevish child who couldn't get his way, taking to his bed and refusing food. Jezebel, having been raised to be a despot, could not understand why Ahab didn't simply *take* what he wanted. She contemptuously offered to handle the problem *for* him. Jezebel did Ahab's dirty work as a power-play, for Ahab was a mere pawn in her game. She was utterly ruthless in her character assassination of Naboth. She caused righteous Naboth to be falsely accused by signing her husband's name to a document she herself wrote. Her false accusations were believed (while her husband laid around doing nothing to stop her), and Naboth was killed. *(1 Kings 21:1-16)*

Jezebel's crowning crime was the murder of Naboth. Her husband rejoiced while taking over Naboth's property, earning her further disdain. She went one step further and had all Naboth's sons stoned, as well. The heirs had to be destroyed to complete her wicked scheme to fully possess the vineyard. YHWH's patience was exhausted. She had defied God, destroying His innocent servant, and now she must pay.

The devil's crowning crime was to trump up false charges and false witnesses to engineer Jesus' death. For that he lost the keys of hell, and death was swallowed up in victory. Because of Ahab and Jezebel's part in the death of Naboth, Elijah prophesied their destruction.

It wasn't just Naboth's vineyard Jezebel was after. *It was God's vineyard.* Naboth's death symbolized a greater slaughter going on in the hearts of men, for he followed YHWH's ancient paths, refusing to yield to the wicked machinations of Jezebel. The heart of the king should belong to YHWH (God) alone. Israel was the betrothed of YHWH, but Jezebel broke this sacred covenant and cost millions of people their eternal salvation. Though she was a *queen*, she was the *servant* of Satan.

Jezebel---bride of Belial

Jezebel was the harlot who led all Israel into new vistas of whoredom through Baal and Ashtoreth worship.

And what concord hath Christ with Belial? or what part hath he that believeth with an infidel? *(2 Corinthians 6:15)*

Belial, in the New Testament, is a proper appellation for Satan, the wicked one, extreme wickedness or destruction. It is also a personification for the system of impure worship connected with the cult of Aphrodite, or Ashtoreth. In the Old Testament it indicated worthlessness, recklessness, lawlessness, wickedness and corruption.

And the men of his city...did as Jezebel had sent unto them... *(1 Kings 21:11)*

Amazingly, the men do her bidding in nefarious activities. Because she is unscrupulous, and the moral waters are thoroughly muddied through idolatry, others gladly follow.

Then THEY sent to Jezebel, saying, Naboth is stoned, and is dead. And it came to pass, when Jezebel heard that Naboth was stoned, and was dead, that Jezebel said to Ahab, Arise, take possession of the vineyard of Naboth. *(1 Kings 21:14-15)*

Notice *they* sent to *Jezebel*, not Ahab, but when *God* wants to speak He sends His prophets to Ahab who is the rightful leader. Jezebel now gives the orders in the kingdom. The death of Naboth's sons is recorded in 2 Kings.

Surely I have seen yesterday the blood of Naboth, and the blood of his sons, saith the LORD... *(2 Kings 9:26)*

Jezebel caused the murder of all Naboth's innocent sons, thereby clearing away any further legal claim to the property. Because the property of the fathers was inherited by the sons, so was guilt according to Hebrew law. She cunningly used this ancient custom to her advantage.

Jezebel has no problem executing anyone who opposes her. She always considers the advancement of her goals more important than the lives of those who live in the society around her. Beware, if you happen to be in the path of a Jezebel!

13

Elijah Confronts Ahab

Elijah told the cowardly Ahab, **"thou hast sold thyself to work evil in the sight of the LORD."** *(1 Kings 21:20)* He prophesied that the dogs would lick the blood of Ahab. Three years later, after Ahab received a mortal wound in battle, his chariot was taken to the spring running through Naboth's vineyards to be washed, and the dogs licked his blood. *(1 Kings 21:19)* Jezebel's fate was also decided: **"The dogs shall eat Jezebel by the wall of Jezreel."** *(1 Kings 21:23)* Additionally, every member of their household would be killed.

Jezebel lived ten years after Ahab's death. She never mourned his death, but continued to weave a web of deception and destruction for Israel through her sons. Jehu defeated her son's army and spoke destruction to the whoredoms of Jezebel. He killed her son, the king, and threw his body into Naboth's vineyard. Determined to die like the defiant queen that she was, she stood in the window and insulted Jehu. He called out, **"Who is on my side? Who?"**

Jezebel was pushed from the window by her eunuchs and trampled by Jehu's horse according to Elijah's word. *(2 Kings 9:35)* Her death was gruesome, gory and grizzly. Her thirty years of tyranny were ended. Ahab's seventy sons were slain, their heads put in baskets and brought to Jehu. Truly, the wages of sin is death.

> **And thou (Elijah) shalt speak unto him (Ahab), saying, Thus saith the LORD, Hast thou killed, and also taken possession? And thou shalt speak unto him, saying, Thus saith the LORD, In the place where dogs licked the blood of Naboth shall dogs lick thy blood, even thine. *(1 Kings 21:19)***

Notice that even though Jezebel concocted the scheme to destroy Naboth and take his vineyard, Ahab, as head of the household and nation was held accountable, and his whole family was punished. The same is true today. Anyone who allows Jezebel to operate will be held accountable.

> **And Ahab said to Elijah, Hast thou found me, O MINE ENEMY? And he answered, I have found thee: because thou hast SOLD thyself to work evil in the sight of the LORD. Behold, I will bring evil upon thee, and will take away thy posterity...** (*1 Kings 21:20-21*)

Elijah catches Ahab red-handed while he is taking possession of the vineyard. Sadly, Ahab considered God's true prophet to be HIS ENEMY, while allowing the false prophets to dine at Jezebel's table. Elijah told Ahab that he had SOLD himself (makar), meaning he made merchandise of himself in the same way as a daughter is sold into marriage or slavery, also it means to surrender or sell away self.

Nothing escaped the LORD's notice. What a contrast Ahab was to King David, who considered God's prophet to be his ally. A curse is on Ahab's descendants. They were all killed because of his sin.

> **And of Jezebel also spake the LORD, saying, The dogs shall eat Jezebel by the wall of Jezreel. Him that dieth of Ahab in the city the dogs shall eat; and him that dieth in the field shall the fowls of the air eat.** (*1 Kings 21:23-24*)

Jezebel's fate was sealed, as well as the rest of Ahab's descendants. She died by the wall of Jezreel and was eaten by dogs. She was not in fear after this prophecy, but chose to trust her evil gods of pride, deception, false bravado, error, lust, covetousness and wickedness.

> **... there was none like unto Ahab, which did sell himself to work wickedness in the sight of the LORD, whom Jezebel his wife STIRRED up. And he did very abominably in following idols...** (*1 Kings 21:25*)

Jezebel inspired Ahab and STIRRED him up through her seductions. YHWH knew Ahab was a victim of the wicked Jezebel,
but this did not excuse his actions.

**And it came to pass, when Ahab heard those words, that he
rent his clothes, and put sackcloth upon his flesh, and fasted,
and lay in sackcloth, and went SOFTLY.** (*1 Kings 21:27*)

Ahab made a great *show* of repentance. A man of malleable
passions, he plunged into the depths of despair, going about
SOFTLY ("at" in Hebrew) meaning a charmer, gently, secretly,
softly. His *appearance* was that of a man who was very, *very* sorry
for getting caught confiscating Naboth's property.

**...because he humbleth himself before Me, I will not
bring the evil in his days: but in his son's days will I
bring the evil upon his house.** (*1 Kings 21:29*)

YHWH had pity on him even then and deferred the killing of
his family until Ahab's death. The fast was a sign of repentance,
though he quickly returned to dishonoring YHWH and His true
prophets. Our God hears sinners and believers alike when they
humble themselves before Him. The power of a holy fast can
even connect an unbeliever with an always merciful, loving
God.
    How can God overlook so much wickedness so easily? The
scriptures show several examples of YHWH's judgment upon a
wicked man or nation being stayed by a fast. Nineveh is a prime
example. When the king and the people repented and fasted,
YHWH delayed their judgment until the time of their descendants.
Nineveh was named after "Nimrod," its founder, the wicked son
and husband of Semiramis.
    Nineveh's fast delayed the judgment of God, as told in the
book of Jonah. Ahab, the most wicked king up to that time in
Israel's history, was reprieved from judgment because he volun-
tarily humbled himself and fasted before YHWH.
    Our God is exceedingly merciful. Knowing this is of critical
importance, for when God has brought someone to the brink of destruction, humbling oneself and fasting is an effective and
desirable attitude of heart. In both Nineveh and in Ahab's case,
they were spared in their own generation, but judgment did arrive
for their descendants.

14

Man's Prophets vs. God's Prophets

Jezebel and Ahab's daughter, Athaliah, married Jehoshaphat's son, Jehoram. Thus, there was an alliance between the kings of Israel and Judah. Jehoshaphat desired to hear prophecy before he and Ahab went into battle together.

> **And Jehoshaphat said unto the king of Israel, Inquire, I pray thee, at the Word of the LORD today.** (*1 Kings 22:5*)

Jehoshaphat meant for Ahab to inquire of the prophets of YHWH, but Ahab sent for his man-pleasing false prophets, instead.

> **Then the king of Israel gathered the prophets together, about four hundred men, and said unto them, Shall I go against Ramoth-gilead to battle, or shall I forbear? And they said, Go up; for the LORD shall deliver it into the hand of the king.** (*1 Kings 22:6*)

The 400 prophets may have been the surviving prophets of Ashtoreth, and would have had to endorse or at least tolerate Baal worship to escape persecution. They probably practiced calf-worship. A lying spirit was in their mouths to instruct the kings, both of whom were out of YHWH's will. Jehoshaphat should never have formed an alliance with the idolatrous Ahab.

> **And Jehoshaphat said, Is there not here a prophet of the LORD, besides, that we might inquire of him?** (*1 Kings 22:7*)

Jehoshaphat did not fail to notice that none of YHWH's prophets were present.

And the king of Israel said unto Jehoshaphat, There is yet one man, Micaiah the son of Imlah, by whom we may inquire of the LORD: but I HATE him; for he doth not prophesy good concerning me, but evil. (1 Kings 22:8)

Ahab HATED the truth and chose to believe a lie. He also hated prophets who spoke truth, calling Elijah his enemy. The same thing is happening in our present day.

Then the king of Israel called an officer, and said, Hasten hither Micaiah the son of Imlah. (*1 Kings 22:9*)

It is possible that Ahab was keeping Micaiah in prison when the officer was sent to fetch him.

...and all the prophets prophesied before them. (*1 Kings 22:10*)

The false prophets were eager to speak and curry the king's favor.

And Zedekiah, the son of Chenaanah made him horns of iron: and he said, Thus saith the LORD, With these shalt thou push the Syrians, until thou have consumed them. (*1 Kings 22:11*)

Zedekiah manifested a spirit of exhibitionism. He was demonstrative but false.

And all the prophets prophesied so, saying, Go up to Ramoth-gilead, and prosper: for the LORD shall deliver it into the king's hand. (*1 Kings 22:12*)

Vanity kicked in and it was impossible for the two kings to hear the truth after these false "words" of encouragement.

And the messenger that was gone to call Micaiah spake unto him saying, Behold now, the words of the prophets declare good unto the king with one mouth... (*1 Kings 22:13*)

The messenger was trying to influence Micaiah to speak good prophecies, also. However, Micaiah was a true prophet and chose God's way over man's way.

And Micaiah said, As the LORD liveth, what the LORD saith unto me, that will I speak. (*1 Kings 22:14*)

This is what every true prophet should say, regardless of the consequences. Unfortunately, many of today's prophets are really "man's" prophets.

And he (Micaiah) said, I saw all Israel scattered upon the hill, as sheep that have not a shepherd: and the LORD said, these have no master: let them return every man to his house in peace. (*1 Kings 22:17*)

Micaiah had prophesied defeat of the armies and Ahab's death. Though YHWH's true prophet spoke, both kings chose to believe the false prophets.

And the king of Israel said unto Jehoshaphat, Did I not tell thee that he would prophesy no good concerning me, but evil? (*1 Kings 22:18*)

Ahab showed contempt for Micaiah and for YHWH, even though Micaiah was the best friend he ever had. Ahab knew, somewhere deep in his heart, that the word of Micaiah was true, but he chose to believe a lie. There are many pastors and their flocks today who would rather hear "words" that flatter and soothe, rather than the truth which may be hard to swallow, and bring great conviction. The truth may be painful, it may not flatter our vanity, but it is much kinder than the lies brought by the deceiver, received by those with itching ears. Ahab made a fatal mistake by not listening to YHWH's true prophet, and paid for it with his life.

A lying spirit came to YHWH and volunteered to lie through the mouths of Ahab's prophets:

Now therefore, behold, the LORD hath put a lying spirit in the mouth of all these THY prophets, and the LORD hath spoken evil concerning thee. (*1 Kings 22:23*)

Notice that Micaiah called the other prophets "his" (Ahab's) prophets. These were "man's" prophets. They spoke only what men wanted to hear, unlike "YHWH's" prophets, who spoke only what God said, even when it meant persecution or death. Micaiah noted that the lying spirit did YHWH's will, yet it was still a lie.

Micaiah is seen as impudent. They probably detect mocking irony in his tone of voice.

But Zedekiah...smote Micaiah on the cheek... (1 Kings 22:24)

This was a terrible insult, but true prophets have always suffered persecution, both from false prophets, and from those who don't want to hear the truth.

...Thus saith the king, Put this fellow in the prison, and feed him with bread of affliction and with water of affliction, until I come in peace. (1 Kings 22:27)

Many true prophets have suffered death rather than lie or deny the truth. The king preferred "his" own man-pleasing prophets.

And Micaiah said, If thou return at all in peace, the LORD hath not spoken by me... (1 Kings 22:28)

Even knowing he will be beaten and tortured he did not recant his statements. He stood alone much as Elijah stood alone on Mount Carmel. Yet he knew, as we must also know in our hearts, that a true prophet never stands alone, but has the power team, Father, Son and Holy Spirit standing with him.

And the king of Israel said unto Jehoshaphat, I will disguise myself, and enter into the battle; but put thou on thy robes... (1 Kings 22:30)

It was incredible that Jehoshaphat agreed to this. A king was certainly a target in his royal robes. Ahab thought he could fool the soldiers and YHWH.

But the king of Syria commanded his thirty and two captains that had rule over his chariots, saying, Fight neither with small nor great, save ONLY WITH THE KING OF ISRAEL. (1 Kings 22:31)

The LORD had surely targeted Ahab for his disobedience and unbelief by having his enemies target **ONLY HIM.**

> **And it came to pass, when the captains of the chariots saw Jehoshaphat, that they said, Surely it is the king of Israel. And they turned aside to fight against him: and Jehoshaphat cried out. And it came to pass, when the captains of the chariots perceived that it was not the king of Israel, that they turned back from pursuing him.** (*1 Kings 22:32-33*)

God was surely protecting him. How else would the captains know for certain that he wasn't Ahab? It is a miracle he wasn't killed due to sheer gullibility.

> **And a certain man drew a bow at a venture, and smote the king of Israel between the joints of the harness...** (*1 Kings 22:34*)

This was YHWH's arrow of judgment. The man was just shooting but Ahab had a divine appointment.

> **And the battle increased that day: and the king was stayed up in his chariot against the Syrians, and died at even: and the blood ran out of the wound into the midst of the chariot.** (*1 Kings 22:35*)

Ahab's death wasn't *accidental*—it was *providential.* Refusing to follow the one true God, he chose the sensuous, wicked life, living with Jezebel in her ivory palace. God's arrow will find *all* who choose a life of sin. Paul the apostle was contented in prison, but Ahab was discontented in a palace.

> **And one washed the chariot in the pool of Samaria; and the dogs licked up his blood...** (*1 Kings 22:38*)

Elijah's prophecy of YHWH's judgment was fulfilled.

15

Jehu: The Revenger of Blood

Several years after Ahab's death, his son Joram was king in Israel. Jezebel was still a force to be reckoned with, giving advice from behind the throne of her wicked son.

Jehu was anointed to be the tenth king of Israel, the first in the fifth dynasty of kings. Jehu means "Jah is he." Twenty years before he began to reign he was divinely singled out as the king of Israel by Elijah. He was anointed by a servant of Elisha when he was still a general in the army.

> ...thou (Jehu) shalt smite the house of Ahab thy master, that I may avenge the blood of my servants the prophets, and blood of all the servants of the LORD, at the hand of Jezebel. (*2 Kings 9:7*)

Jehu received this prophecy from YHWH declaring him to be the revenger of blood for Naboth and his family. In the Old Testament an avenger of blood was a name given to a man who had the right to take revenge on him who had killed one of his relations.

> And the dogs shall eat Jezebel in the portion of Jezreel, and there shall be none to bury her. (*2 Kings 9:10*)

This is a repeat of Elijah's prophecy concerning Jezebel, given to Jehu to carry out. Following this prophecy, Jehu went to Jezreel to carry out the LORD's directions, and destroyed Baal worship in the process.

Is it peace, Jehu?

Jehu came "furiously" to cleanse the land of the wickedness of Jezebel and her son, Joram, who was king.

> **And the watchman told, saying, He came even unto them, and cometh not again: and the driving is like the driving of Jehu the son of Nimshi; for he driveth FURIOUSLY.** *(2 Kings 9:20)*

Jehu came FURIOUSLY because he was YHWH's instrument of wrath, driven by **THE KING**.

There is no peace with Jezebel

> **And it came to pass, when Joram (king of Israel) saw Jehu, that he said, Is it peace, Jehu? And he answered, What peace, so long as the whoredoms of thy mother Jezebel and her witchcrafts are so many?** *(2 Kings 9:22)*

Where there is witchcraft, there is only turmoil and confusion. Jezebel's witchcrafts were many and she was still fully operational with her sorceries at this time. The sins of the parents came down on Joram who inherited generational curses.

> **And Joram turned his hands, and fled, and said to Ahaziah, There is treachery, O Ahaziah. And Jehu drew a bow with his full strength, and smote Jehoram between his arms, and the arrow went out at his heart, and he sunk down in his chariot.** *(2 Kings 9:23-24)*

Jezebel's son, Joram, ran for his life, but Jehu drew back his bow and shot him through the heart. Be assured, if you follow Jezebel, you have an appointment with eternal death. Jehu's arrow was divinely guided, just as David's smooth stone was supernaturally guided into Goliath's forehead, and the arrow that killed Ahab, even though he was disguised, was divinely guided. Anyone who follows Jezebel will have the same fate. Their wicked, idolatrous hearts will ultimately condemn them to death. The aim of the LORD is sure. The wicked will surely perish and the Word of the LORD will be fulfilled.

> Then said Jehu to Bidkar his captain, Take up, and
> cast him in the portion of the field of Naboth the
> Jezreelite: for remember how that, when I and thou
> rode together after Ahab his father, the LORD laid this
> burden upon him; Surely I have seen yesterday the
> blood of Naboth, and the blood of his sons, saith the
> LORD; and I will requite thee in this plat, saith the
> LORD. Now therefore take and cast him into the plat of
> ground, according to the Word of the LORD. (2 Kings
> 9:25-26)

He was tossed into the same plot of ground belonging to
Naboth.

> But when Ahaziah the king of Judah saw this, he
> fled by the way of the garden house. And Jehu followed
> after him and said, Smite him also in the chariot, And
> they did so... (2 Kings 9:27)

Jehu slew two kings—- Joram and Ahaziah—-in one fell
swoop. Joram, Jezebel's son and king of Israel, and Ahaziah,
Jezebel's grandson, king of Judah, killed by happenstance
because he was hanging out with the wrong crowd. Bad company
can get you killed.

16

Jezebel's Eunuchs

All who follow Jezebel become her eunuchs. She strips men of their manhood, and men and women of their free will.

> **And when Jehu was come to Jezreel, Jezebel heard of it; and she painted her face, and tired (dressed) her head, and looked out at a window.** (*2 Kings 9:30*)

Meanwhile, even in her final scene, Jezebel was trying to manipulate the situation to her advantage. Though she had a grandson who was twenty-three years old, she dressed her hair and painted her face and eyes to make them appear more brilliant, still thinking she could seduce and captivate men with her charms. She looked (seductively) out her window as Jehu, having just killed her son, arrived. She taunted him, determined to go to her death as a queen. Even at the end, though she must have suspected the danger, she was arrogant, trying to use deception and seduction on Jehu.

> **And as Jehu entered in at the gate, she said, Had Zimri peace, who slew his master?** (*2 Kings 9:31*)

Zimri, to whom she referred, was a general who rebelled, killed his king and usurped the throne of Israel, killing the king's whole family and their friends. He only reigned seven days. Omri, Ahab's father, who was a general in Israel's army, took over. Zimri burned himself in the palace along with all his possessions. Omri then became king. Jezebel brought up Zimri's name to imply that Jehu would end up like Zimri, and therefore he should pander to her.

And he lifted up his face to the window, and said, WHO IS ON MY SIDE? WHO? And there looked out to him two or three eunuchs. (*2 Kings 9:32*)

These words echo down through the centuries. WHO IS ON THE LORD'S SIDE? We must make a choice: Now or never! We must throw Jezebel down and smash her stronghold over our lives. Are we Jezebel's eunuch's? Or are we vital servants of YHWH?

Turning men into eunuch's by castration is strictly against God's Word. *(Deuteronomy 23)* This practice was begun by the wicked queen, Semiramis, originator of pagan religions, who wanted servants who excited no jealousy.

And he said, Throw her down. So they threw her down; and some of her blood was sprinkled on the wall, and on the horses: and he trode her under foot. (*2 Kings 9:33*)

The eunuch's waked, as if from slumber, after being under the spell of a wicked queen, and became instruments in YHWH's plan. We, too, must awaken from slumber and regain our courage. Jehu did what God will do to all those who follow Jezebel. Now is the time to repent and cast Jezebel out! Queen mothers were usually treated with more dignity, but in Jezebel's case, an exception was made.

And when he was come in, he did eat and drink, and said, Go, see now this cursed woman, and bury her: for she is a king's daughter. (*2 Kings 9:34*)

Once Jezebel was cast out, nothing remained except a reminder that we are but a moment away from sin ourselves. We must resist the temptation to **TAKE UP JEZEBEL'S BODY** (her influence), her ways, her idolatry, or treat her memory with honor by worshiping her or her gods.

YHWH ordained that she was not to be revered with a queen's burial. She was the daughter of Satan, Belial, pagan religion, demon spirits, a destroyer of millions, a bad influence, spawn of evil and a progenitor of wickedness. God didn't allow anything to remain of her, according to Elijah's prophecy, except those parts that spoke of her wickedness.

Some think that the reason Jehu sat down to eat and drink a hearty meal after killing Jezebel was to secure a covenant with the town's people through communal ceremony, to bind the people to his leadership (25), but the truth is, he was a rough soldier and a crude man, **COMPLETELY WITHOUT PITY**. In other words, *he was the perfect man to deal with Jezebel.*

> **And they went to bury her: but they found no more of her than the SKULL, and the FEET, and the PALMS of her hands. Wherefore they came again, and told him (Jehu). And he said, This is the Word of the LORD, which He spake by His servant Elijah the Tishbite, saying, In the portion of Jezreel shall dogs eat the flesh of Jezebel...** (*2 Kings 9:35-36*)

The prophecy was fulfilled as spoken by Elijah.

> **And the carcass of Jezebel shall be as dung upon the face of the field in the portion of Jezreel; so that they shall not say, This is Jezebel.** (*2 Kings 9:37*)

It was important that she not be honored by a queen's burial. Her followers might have worshipped or revered her as they did Queen Semiramis, her precursor, had there been a grave site.

God's true servants will not be seduced by Jezebel. She will surely fall to her death. Her wickedness will be trampled out in the wine press of the wrath of Almighty God, just as Jehu's horse crushed her under its feet in the vineyard of Naboth. Nothing will remain of her wickedness. Queen Jezebel was thrown to her death by traitors in her *own* court. (Jezebel beware, your wickedness will find you out, and your own followers, with whom you have conspired in your wicked deeds, will betray you.) The dogs ate her flesh. All that was left were the palms of her hands, feet and skull. Elaboration on this significance follows:

- Hands: represent works, guilt, idolatry, weakness.
- Feet: stand for heart, offense, stubbornness, unbelief, sin.
- Hands and feet: Yahshua was nailed in both hands and feet to provide deliverance for our souls.
- Skull: (Golgatha) place of the skull where Yahshua Messiah was crucified, and the place where *we* are to be crucified.

The dogs left behind the parts of Jezebel that speak a warning to us: Keep your hands and heart pure and walk only in the paths of YHWH. Allow your hands and feet to be nailed to the cross of the true Messiah, and crucify your flesh and your mind at the place of the skull.

Naboth's death was avenged. Jezebel, her son and grandsons were slain in Jezreel where Naboth lived and had his vineyard. Joram's body was tossed into Naboth's vineyard and Jezebel's scarlet blood was splattered against her precious ivory palace and on the ground where she was thrown from a window. She was eaten by dogs in the same field she conspired to take from Naboth, a fitting end to a blood-thirsty career.

> **...take ye the heads of the men your master's sons, and come to me...Now the king's sons, being seventy persons...** (*2 Kings 10:6*)

The people killed all of Ahab's sons at Jehu's command, just as Jezebel killed all of Naboth's sons.

> **So Jehu slew all that remained of the house of Ahab in Jezreel...** (*2 Kings 10:11*)

The book is closed on the house of Ahab. YHWH was long-suffering, but in the end, since none truly repented, none were saved.

Sadly, after all his success as YHWH's avenger, Jehu went back to the calf-worship that Jeroboam had established.

A vigorous and vigilant watch must be maintained if men of God are to continue a set-apart (holy—kodesh) walk. All too many men and women fall to the wiles, temptations and schemes of the devil after experiencing great success: King Saul did, Jehu did, David did, and many men and women in our contemporary culture have yielded to the temptations of the pride of life and the lusts of the flesh.

I was recently consulted and asked to pray for a large worldwide ministry that discovered it was headed up by a man with a Jezebel spirit. The leaders under him had become faint-hearted, engulfed with lethargy. Under Jezebel's control they suffered emotional and spiritual abuse, and subsequently languished in condemnation. They were relentlessly brainwashed into believing it was all their own fault, and the constant rain of accusations served to rob them of their sense of identity. Several of these godly and passionate men and women were so discouraged they have either quit or are thinking of quitting.

Meanwhile, Jezebel voraciously tore down years of carefully planned work by publically denouncing groups with established relationships to their organization. JEHUS AND ELIJAHS ARISE! It takes bold saints full of the Holy Ghost, moving in the forerunner spirit of Elijah, to withstand Jezebel.

Part Three

The Jezebel Spirit

And I gave her space to repent of her fornication; and she repented not. *Revelation 2:21*

17

The Wicked Witch of the North

Jezebel personified

The Jezebel persona is unique, thus we will deal with it uniquely. This evil spirit took the form of an actual human being. Jezebel, after all, was a real flesh and blood person, possessed of a wicked spirit who took her name and continues on, making a special reappearance now, at the end of the age.

> ...because thou sufferest that woman Jezebel, which calleth herself a prophetess, to teach and to seduce my servants to commit fornication... Behold, I will cast her into a bed, and them that commit adultery with her into GREAT TRIBULATION except they repent of their deeds. And I will kill her children with death; and all the churches shall know that I am He which searcheth the reins and hearts: and I will give unto every one of you according to your works. (*Revelation 2:20-23*)

Jezebel's profile

A person with a Jezebel spirit has a combination of wicked spirits working together: This person has a controlling spirit, a spirit of seduction, a spirit of slumber, an antichrist spirit, a spirit of whoredoms, a spirit of deception, a spirit of haughtiness and pride, a lying spirit, a spirit of error, covetousness and lusts of the flesh, a spirit of murder, a spirit of witchcraft and divination, and has gone a step further to receive a Jezebel spirit.

Jezebel uses familiar spirits to inform her of her opponent's and victim's activities. People with controlling spirits can be brought around, but a person with a *true* Jezebel spirit has gone almost too far to repent: She rarely repents! (26) Once she develops a taste for power and blood, she is unwilling to relinquish it.

Weak in her presence

The Jezebel spirit is so powerful that in its presence one feels weak. I've seen people become lethargic, helpless, sometimes unable to move limbs or speak coherently, except in a zombie or drone-like way, the effect lasting after the person with the Jezebel spirit has long gone. The strong antichrist spirit that works through Jezebel seeks to silence (Jezebel killed) the true prophets. A person with this spirit will never admit he/she is wrong but will manifest a controlling spirit, gone off the deep end, out of control. YHWH's people want to run like Elijah, but under Jezebel they become more like her eunuchs than mighty men and women of valor.

18

Notes On How To Rule From An Ivory Palace

The ruins of Ahab's ivory palace were uncovered in Samaria. The walls had been faced with ivory and thousands of pieces of exquisitely carved inlaid panels and plaques, cabinets and couches were found. (27) Yet all his riches could not save him, for he turned his back on YHWH to go whoring after Baal. He yielded his spiritual authority to Jezebel, and she ruled him and his kingdom from within the palace walls.

First, it goes without saying that the imperious Jezebel will never mingle with the great unwashed, unless there is no other way to handle a problem. Let the underlings carry out the dirty work. She never comes down to the level of those she rules. She remains aloof in her ivory palace. She commands while hiding behind others. She threatens Elijah, yet never faces him. She plots against Naboth, yet never gets her own hands stained with his blood. She mocks Jehu, yet remains aloof, looking out the window of her ivory palace.

Second, it takes a traitor from within her ranks to bring her downfall. Jezebel maintains informants who apprise her of whatever is going on. Additionally, what people can't overhear, familiar spirits can. This is how she knows so much about people and their affairs, yet she herself seems untouchable.

Jezebel "stirs up" a poisonous stew

Jezebel knew how to "stir up" her victims. She manipulated her husband, everyone and everything around her.

> **But there was none like unto Ahab, which did SELL himself to work wickedness in the sight of the LORD, whom Jezebel his wife STIRRED up. (*1 Kings 21:26*)**

The word "stirred" (cuwth) means seduce, stimulate, inspire, soothe, entice, persuade, provoke, stir up. The word "sell" (makar) means sell away oneself into slavery or marriage. Jezebel seduces her victims into slavery to false gods and idols of wealth, perversion, power and possession. Additionally, she slaughters the innocent and the righteous who stand against her.

Jezebel dominates with a controlling spirit

Jezebel walks in dominance, surrounded by bitter envyings and a constant atmosphere of confusion. Jezebel finds it difficult to delegate authority. She gives orders, but won't allow them to be carried out without humiliating the other person involved. Then, she takes back the authority. If she delegates, she retracts it, unable to allow others to function in positions of responsibility. She belittles and gossips, operating in bitter envying and strife.

Jezebel uses anger or silence to control. This is witchcraft. Jezebel tries to control pastors and churches. Some pastors have this spirit, and through it they seek to control their congregations. Some Jezebels manipulate from behind the scenes while others are blatant and in your face. Jezebel won't get along with anyone she can't dominate. When in the presence of a Jezebel spirit, one fervently wishes to be elsewhere. Sometimes a horrible creepy-crawly sensation permeates the atmosphere. When leaving, one just wants to take a shower. Yuk!

The strange attraction

Some people are attracted to Jezebel's company and find amusement through her as she/he ridicules others with her rapier wit. She engages in sarcasm, mocking friend and foe alike. Those who are attracted to her for this should take heed, for she will turn on them as well, like a viper, without pity or feeling. Husbands who submit to a wife with a Jezebel spirit beware, for she is like a black widow spider: She will kill and slowly suck the life out of her mate.

Jezebel dominates others by her vanity, hatred, disdain, insecurity and jealousy. She publicly humiliates others, including spouses. With the tongue she wrecks, demeans and destroys. Through character assassination, she makes others fearful of her sharp tongue, willing to compromise in order to avoid the tongue-lashings. Jezebel questions the manhood or ability of others, making them feel small. Jezebel is the cause of many divorces. A married person with this spirit will drive his or her spouse to sink into alcohol, TV, adultery, material success, bury themselves in their work, social clubs, church, the children, excessive golf or other sports, sleep, or the newspaper to escape the wrath of Jezebel's tongue.

Jezebel lives in conflict

Rebellion plays a key role with Jezebel. She sows seeds of unrest. She lives in conflict. She tries to control, arrange, and dominate everyone around her. She keeps others in a state of turmoil. Jezebel often targets women who are embittered against men. (28) From her heart she yields to no one, even though for public appearances she will seem to do so, in order to rule through another. Jezebel attacks suddenly, without warning. She is vicious, unrelenting and pitiless, and she is an exceptionally fine actor. But remember, she won't live with anyone she can't dominate.

If Jezebel is not in control of a meeting, she may stand up and interrupt or badger the speaker with irrelevant questions, or find something to stridently take issue with in order to disrupt, sometimes using loud accusations.

Jezebel the predator

Jezebel is very shark-like in her nature. All sharks do is swim and eat. They feed on the weak and sick. Jezebel cruises up and down the halls of her ivory palace, waiting to pounce on Ahab or any other hapless victim. When Ahab shows the slightest weakness, she finishes him. She ruthlessly takes the kingdom from him during one of his pouting, pity parties. She destroys the lives of all who get in her path and interfere with her ambitions.

Jezebel preys on the weak

Jezebel attempts to seduce and produce dirt on those in authority who have exploitable weakness of the flesh (pastors, bosses, opposing political parties, etc.). Later, she uses this information to control or destroy her victims. If they won't yield to her manipulations, she eliminates them or their credibility through exposing their weaknesses and their nefarious deeds.

Bedroom blackmail

Jezebel often uses the power of sexual passion to control. A Jezebel sometimes turns his/her spouse into little more than a helpless slave who submits to the perverse demons that operate through Jezebel. Often, she will manipulate her victims through sexual favors, or withheld sexual favors. She then holds her victims through fear of exposure. I heard of a pastor and wife who taped counseling sessions, and then used this information to hold a whole church hostage.

Jezebel controls through perversion

Jezebel often controls her/his spouse through addiction to perversion. The victim feels helpless to escape, and may be deceived into performing various forms of perversion. Jezebel sometimes seeks to defile through pornography, lulling her victims into gradual, ever harder exposure. This is prevalent in our homes, businesses, churches and nation.

Jezebel seeks worship

Jezebel seeks to be worshipped, using sorcery and manipulation. She will not tolerate anyone who wants to serve the true God, YHWH. She uses deception, divination and witchcraft to turn the people's hearts away from YHWH. Her tools are greed, pornography, idolatry, sins of the flesh, etc.

Recently, I was asked to speak at a church where the pastor's wife has a Jezebel spirit. She rules the roost and he goes along with it. She teaches the women that they do not have to be submitted to their husbands; in fact, she encourages open rebellion and a spirit of independence. The women's meetings have turned into shocking twists of scripture and man-bashing, reminiscent of the early feminist movement. A godly woman I know was forced out of the church for taking a stand for righteousness and stating that she loves her husband and follows his leading. The men in this church are sadly beat down and unable to function as heads of their households. All is chaos. When the pastors found out that I teach from the Biblical point of view they called and canceled my invitation to speak, fearful of exposure.

Another church that has a pastor and wife with Jezebel/Ahab spirits, takes groups to the lake on weekend retreats where they get drunk, openly practicing fornication, adultery and wife-swapping. The pastors lead their flock to believe that it's all right. Apparently, people with itching ears will believe *anything* that promotes and encourages their carnal lusts.

Abuse and familiar spirits—spirit of murder

Jezebel operates using familiar spirits. She/he knows what's going on whether present or not. A person who is married to someone with a Jezebel spirit will live in fear, because the familiar spirits relay information to Jezebel. One woman who is married to a minister with a Jezebel spirit was very fearful after confessing that he beat her. She spoke through tears, "Oh no! Now I've told you he beats me and he'll know I told you. He always knows what I say when he's not here. I'm so scared, because he will beat me more, now!" What she didn't know was that others had secretly noted her blackened eyes and frightened, abused appearance.

Jezebel abuses as a way to control. Jezebel desires to destroy others, and the abuse is simply an outlet for the spirit of murder that dwells in Jezebel, expressed through rage. Wife beating (secret or otherwise) is common with the Jezebel spirit. Likewise, emotional, verbal and mental abuse is common with Jezebels of both genders.

Ministering to a person with a Jezebel spirit

When trying to minister to a person with a Jezebel spirit, the person may: sit steaming in silence; refuse to listen; plot revenge. He/she may lash out with a vicious counter-attack that is both vengeful and devastating. A well-advanced Jezebel can *pretend* to receive prayer, even receive prophecies with the appropriate etiquette of an innocent, truth-seeking child of God. She may sit for long periods pretending to receive ministry, then suddenly and inexplicably react violently to something that is said, take up offense against the person who is attempting to minister to her, and leave enraged and indignant. (Watch for sarcastic remarks and sharing of dirt gathered against others, particularly those she wishes to destroy, which she casually drops like juicy tidbits, hoping to lure the unsuspecting into her rumor mill.)

Spiritual Vampirism

Some Jezebels go from meeting to meeting demanding to be the focus of attention. They want to be prayed for "if" that will put all the spotlight on them, and use up the time of the ministers. She will exhaust the counselors or ministers, then move on to another meeting, and another. Jezebel must feed her desperate craving for attention and control. A tell-tale sign is that she never seems to get better.

Jezebel will suck you dry until you're drained of energy. Some Jezebels have a method of pursuit so relentless that if they fail at their first attempt to destroy a meeting, they will lie down and sleep (even snore loudly), then wake up and demand prayer, If they succeed in disrupting in this way they will monopolize the remainder of the meeting, pretending to receive ministry, wearing everyone out. Jezebel brings confusion.

Finally, Jezebel will invariably find something to take offense at, and leave in a huff, energized, while everyone else remains drained. She may even express anger at the minister for wasting her time. One key is knowing, in advance, that Jezebel *will* turn on anyone sincerely trying to minister to her, and launch an attack.

19
Jezebel Seeks Destruction of the Prophets

Jezebel has the distinction of being the first female persecutor in history. Jezebel's true enemy is the prophet of God. She hates the prophets and seeks to kill them just as she murdered hundreds of them in Israel.

A true prophet will lead the people to repentance and humility. Jezebel hates repentance, humility and prayer. She seeks to stir the people up against the true prophets in order to kill and silence the prophetic, because a true prophet will expose Jezebel for who she is. This is why Jezebel always seeks to control pastors, leaders, presidents, the goings on in churches, and persecute the prophets who speak the truth.

Jezebel's ultimate hatred is against God, Himself

If Jezebel controls a pastor, she will run all the true prophets off, for she fears exposure. She causes fear and discouragement in God's prophets just as she did in Elijah and John the Baptist. *(1 Kings 19:4)* Even after his great victory on Mount Carmel, when Jezebel threatened him, Elijah ran away in fear and suffered an attack of heaviness, self recrimination and depression, praying that he might die. While John the Baptist languished in prison he began to doubt that Yahshua was the Messiah, sending his followers to question Yahshua concerning His divinity. *(Luke 7:19)*

Jezebel often poses as a prophet (she is a false prophet)

Jezebel calls herself a prophetess *(Revelation 2:20)* and tries to align herself with prophets. Jezebel will claim to intercede but never does. Jezebel usurps authority. There may be displays of intense anger and fits thrown in order to manipulate and control. She will flatter her victims first to win them over, then treacherously turns against them.

> **But there were false prophets also among the people, even as there shall be false teachers among you, who privily shall bring in damnable heresies ...and many shall follow their pernicious ways...** (*2 Peter 2:1-2*)

If Jezebel wants to eliminate someone from the picture who is a threat to her/him, she will *"have a vision or dream"* about the person and then falsely accuse the person of inappropriate speech or actions. Those who believe and support Jezebel will choose to believe her falsehoods rather than the truth. They will be *too fearful* to do what is right, and stand by the person who is under the false attack. Battles against Jezebel can only be won by warring in the Spirit, *never* the flesh. Attempts to establish your own righteousness will utterly fail. Do not run in fear! Let YHWH defend you!

> **Notwithstanding the LORD stood with me, and strengthened me...and I was delivered out of the mouth of the lion. And the LORD shall deliver me from every evil work, and will preserve me unto His heavenly kingdom...** (*2 Timothy 4:17-18*)

Jezebel is "man's" prophet

Jezebel speaks false prophecies for the purpose of manipulating and producing followers. She enjoins her victims to follow her, leading them down the path to destruction by prophesying personal, financial or business success, which often blows up in their faces.

Because of these prophecies, Jezebel has many *devotees* who blindly follow her/him around like puppies, ignoring inaccuracy in theology and grossly failed prophecies, such as: prophesying that someone will die within a certain time frame (upsetting everyone involved terribly), or prophesying that there will be a tremendous amount of money (the Brinks Truck is coming!), or prophesying a terrific business deal will ensue (they usually wind up destitute, business failed). Jezebel's prophecies are often fanciful, not biblically based, but they *"sound"* good. It takes great discernment to wade through the biblio-babble to arrive at the truth.

> **For the time will come when they will not endure SOUND doctrine; but after their own lusts shall they heap to themselves teachers, having itching ears; And they shall turn away their ears from the truth, and shall be turned unto fables.** (*2 Timothy 4:3-4*)

When the prophecies fail to come to pass, all the followers of Jezebel *get busy* (including Jezebel herself) making excuses to explain the fiasco away. Jezebel always has excuses, excuses, excuses.

The victims are usually so flattered and deceived by the attention of receiving personal prophecies that they will do *anything* to excuse away Jezebel's flaws. Others, lamentably, are crushed and fall away from their faith, embittered and wounded.

> **Let no man deceive you by any means: for that day shall not come, except there come a falling away first...** *(2 Thessalonians 2:3)*

The big catch is that some of Jezebel's prophecies are correct, *just enough* to keep her followers coming back. She/he uses familiar spirits and divination to deliver a certain amount of accuracy. To test the prophecy, look at the prophet's lifestyle, look at the fruit, look at the track record, look at the personality and character. To test the spirit, ask, "Is Jesus Christ (Yahshua Messiah) come in the flesh?" *(1 John 4:2)* To test a man ask, "Is Jesus Christ LORD?" *(1 John 4:15)*

> **But evil men and seducers (impostors) shall wax worse and worse (go from bad to worse), deceiving, and being deceived.** (*2 Timothy 3:13*)

Prophets who operate in mixture

Some Jezebel's operate in *mixture*, too. That is, they are *partly* on target and *partly* off. This is because YHWH once gave them a genuine gift that has become tainted and twisted through sin, greed, or lust for power and control. You will not be able to discern the difference unless you are paying close attention to the preaching, teaching, lifestyle and ultimate results.

The ones in mixture are often prophets who desperately need a generous dose of humility and repentance. Usually, there is unresolved sin in their lives. These Jezebels prophesy sometimes in the flesh, sometimes out of envy, jealousy and strife, using what I call "attack prophecies," aimed at correcting whoever Jezebel is mad at. This type of prophecy is divination (witchcraft). Frequently, a spirit of exhibitionism is in operation, too. He/she wants to put on a "show," regardless of accuracy.

Show biz prophets

These "show biz" prophets are not hard to spot. There is no sincerity. Recently, I witnessed a "show biz prophet" spotting people in the congregation whom he wanted to manipulate into giving large amounts to his ministry. He did a dramatic, *very loud* sermon, then called up his "marks," and prophesied great things over them, while shoving one down to his knees; others he pushed over by force. Immediately after they got up he prophesied that someone would give him $300, and that others would give $100 each. Then he took up the offering.

Pushing people over is inappropriate. What is the purpose, if not to exalt the person ministering, and their power over others? If someone is slain in the Spirit, by the Spirit, great!!! I love to see God work in this way. Often, He will minister to them dramatically while they are "fallen under THE POWER." But to deliberately force people to fall backward, or worse, shove them to their knees in a subservient position while ministering to them, is reprehensible.

In Biblical times there were schools for the prophets to provide assistance and help avoid serious mistakes. Now there is little training available. None of this is, in *any* way, an indictment against young fledging (true) prophets, who in their zeal to serve YHWH nearly always make mistakes as they move forward in their training.

Jezebel gathers large offerings

Jezebel wears her victims out with long sermons that go nowhere except straight up to the ***big moment of the evening***—the offering. The offerings are often large because she/he essentially hypnotizes victims with mesmerizing speeches. Everything done is programmed to elicit the desired response: large offerings.

And through covetousness shall they with feigned words make merchandise of you... *(2 Peter 2:3)*

The amazing result is that even though Jezebel's followers wander aimlessly about, extolling the greatness of their leader, believing that their leader's words are golden and straight from God's mouth (a follower actually said this to me), declaring that their leader has the one true message for their area or for this time, they, themselves, are usually fraught with failure and despair.

If the Jezebel spirit operates through a man, women will flock to his "ministry," many of them with "marital problems." Jezebel will string them along while they are useful in spreading his/her "gospel" and/or if finances can be extorted from them.

Jezebel is a wolf in sheep's clothing

Jezebel teaches false religion and bondage in order to gain control.

Beware of false prophets, which come to you in sheep's clothing, but inwardly they are RAVENING wolves. *(Matthew 7:15)*

"Ravening" (harpax) means extortion, taking by force, plundering. Jezebel plunders God's house by taking followers who are easily manipulated into doing her bidding. Jezebel will destroy those who oppose her. She will be heard to say things like, "That's *my* town (church, etc.). No one can take it from me!"

A few years ago a Jezebel got several of her followers to launch a public attack against a true prophetess. I call it a "hag attack." One after the other spoke scathing words against her as she sat in shock at the relentless fury of the assault. The Jezebel in charge finally stopped it after four of her "trainees" had decimated their victim. Since then, I have heard reports of this happening all over the country.

Jezebel attempts to kill or remove detractors

One pastor told me that when a certain person comes to town (who has a Jezebel spirit) the pastor gets sick, nearly dying each time. This is witchcraft, plain and simple. My counsel was for intercessors to pray around the clock, covering this pastor who was a target (since refusing to have Jezebel back to the church) and pray for the city which was grossly defiled and further infested by the Jezebel spirit.

In another incident, one man, an elder who stood up against Jezebel (operating through the pastor's wife and two on the elder board) tried to speak and read scripture at the board meeting. He was told, "You can't come into this board meeting quoting *scripture!*" Strange behavior for a church meeting! When he refused to resign, they attempted to dig up dirt on him concerning his business dealings, and failing that, two of the Jezebel infested board members tried to vote him out.

He went to the pastor to discuss it, but the pastor sat fidgeting, unable to answer him without furtively looking at his wife for her permission to speak. He cowered behind his desk as she controlled the conversation. The elder quit and within two weeks the church imploded on itself and dissolved. It should be noted that just before these incidents, the ministry to the local people had just moved into full swing with outreaches, street ministry and feeding the poor. Jezebel fights against God's work by infiltrating and attempting to destroy churches from within.

Other busy Jezebels go around to many meetings, disrupting them by pretending to *always* have a "word." This "word" invariably draws attention to the speaker, not to YHWH, and is soulish in nature.

Once, when I was new in the ministry, I was speaking at a women's meeting when my heavenly Father directed me to begin ministering deliverance to women with depression. About twenty women came forward and I began walking up and down amongst them, quietly playing my flute. Many were being gloriously set free by the Holy Ghost when suddenly a woman (who I discovered later no one had seen before) began loudly taking over. She noisily dragged out a chair, grabbed a woman who needed healing, sat her down and began shouting at her. I was astonished. The anointing immediately left and the meeting shut down. I have learned that Satan will send in his servants in an attempt to disrupt what God is doing.

At another meeting in a church, a huge man with a Jezebel spirit and a spirit of murder got in my face and began attempting to assault me through point of contact and cursing words. He challenged me in a very menacing and threatening way. I backed away (notice I did not turn my back) and began to pray, for this person had attempted to lay hands on *me* and prophesy. The assault was thwarted. My husband and another friend stepped in between us and I quietly prayed, casting out of the man and the building the wicked spirits that had tried to assault me and destroy the meeting. I pleaded the blood of Yahshua Messiah over everything, and resumed ministering. He, and the Jezebel spirit, left immediately. However, the real Jezebel stronghold resided in the pastor's wife. She was enraged that many were being healed and delivered. In an attempt to stop, or at least disrupt the move of God, she went back and released all the children to race into the sanctuary and grab their parents. But when the congregation refused to leave, she stormed out.

Jezebel frequently attempts to take over meetings that are not hers to direct. She usurps authority. I was asked to minister at a meeting out of town. When I arrived, a person with a Jezebel spirit, began bragging loudly to anyone who would listen about what a great speaker and minister *she* was.

I began the meeting with worship, planning to move into the message and a time of ministry, but "stirred up" with insane jealousy, Jezebel began to dance furiously up and down right in front of me, working herself into a sweaty frenzy. She had a captive audience for everyone was stunned. Then, she began to loudly prophesy for an hour and a half, until she achieved total chaos. Those in charge were so astonished they did nothing; others actually thought this was a move of the Holy Spirit.

And they that are Christ's have crucified the flesh with the affections and lusts. If we live in the Spirit, let us also walk in the Spirit. Let us not be desirous of vain glory, provoking one another, envying one another. (*Galatians 5:24-26*)

Jezebel loves to take over meetings and draw attention to herself. When provoked, she will rail incessantly against you, taking particular care to denigrate whatever YHWH is doing through you with terrible false accusations, then mock you with scriptural principles such as, "Do you *still* love me?" If you try to respond to her attack with sensible words, she will not and cannot listen. She may raise her voice to drown you out. Just pray.

But if ye bite and devour one another, take heed that ye be not consumed one of another. (*Galatians 5:15*)

If Jezebel is present when you are ministering to others, she will interrupt with irrelevant chatter or deliberate distraction to break the anointing. If you *must* be with someone who has a Jezebel spirit, that is, if she manifests in a relative you must associate with, someone you live with or work with, or who goes to your church, bind the spirit of Jezebel in Jesus' Name. Command it to be silent. Be polite to the person but be firm in dealing with this wicked spirit.

In relationship to her own progeny, Jezebel is demanding, perfectionistic and controlling. She/he will attempt to micro-manage everything. Jezebel will never be satisfied with her/his child's performance. If their hair is long, she will tell them they look terrible, and when they cut it short to please her, she will lament about how beautiful it was long. She will assist them and push them to go into a career (often one they don't want), and when they do she will persistently undermine their confidence, throwing in nasty barbs about their performance. If they fail to enter her choice of career, she will never, never let them live it down. If they fail, it is an open door for more criticism.

She will denigrate their choice in a mate and viciously demean their ability as a parent. No matter what Jezebel's child does, it will never be good enough. The child will invariably have low self-image, which will be used against him/her to ridicule the child until finally they are driven in one of several ways: suicide, runaways, anorexia, bulimia, drugs or other escape prone addictions, constant sense of failure, rejection, bitterness, or unforgiveness.

Queen Jezebel ruled from behind the throne of her husband and her sons, never allowing them to escape from her wicked grasp. Modern day Jezebels manipulate to retain control, too. They keep their children in a state of dependency through low self-image which Jezebel has cultivated in them from infancy. Jezebel will use her grandchildren to assault her own children. She will inform her children of all their failures in child rearing while playing up to the grandchildren to create sycophants.

Jezebel loves to use money and possessions to control her children and others. She will make threats about the inheritance, intimidating the children into following orders, often leaving the inheritance to grandchildren or others out of spite. A man I know had a mother with a Jezebel spirit who railed against her adult children for not doing as she desired, frequently threatening to disinherit them for not coming to see her often enough. When she died recently, they discovered she had actually disinherited them all several times, but reinstated them just before death.

One of her daughters, who lived right across the street, had not spoken to her mother in twenty years. She got a very small inheritance, even less than the grandchildren. When she found this out she threw all the plants from the funeral out in the street and caused a traffic jam. This daughter had the same Jezebel spirit her mother had before her, and her bitterness was eating her and her relationships alive.

If Jezebel controls the boss or the superiors on the job, watch out! She/he will force underlings to do her/his will, no matter how outrageous. If a Christian works under Jezebel, great lengths will be taken to humiliate and destroy the Christian's reputation to get them fired. No attack will be too petty or far-fetched.

When I was teaching summer school, a fellow teacher who was possessed of a Jezebel spirit began inciting her students, who came in my class after the break, to be disruptive and to have their parents call the school to try to get me fired. A Christian student in my homeroom told me about it and I went straight to the principal, then confronted the teacher. She denied it of course, but I refused to take her students again.

The following regular school year, I had to come in her classroom while substituting. She assaulted me verbally in front of students and tried to slam my hand in a drawer. Following this, she attempted to get me fired on my first day. The principal was intimidated by her because her mother was on the school board, but to his credit, he kept me on as a long term substitute. This teacher and her mother are holding the whole district hostage, and there are many witches and satanists on staff, and in principal's offices throughout the district.

One principal with a Jezebel spirit in the district tried everything to get another Christian teacher fired. Lies were fabricated and students were used in collusion with the plot to fire this teacher. He was put on suspension with pay and when he called me I told him to rejoice! He retired two months later with full pay.

One friend of mine worked under a manager who triple checked her work, going over and over it trying to find something wrong. She forced my friend to come in early every morning and stay late for no extra pay. She made up phony accusations and had her called on the carpet repeatedly. My friend discovered that this woman hated her because she was a Christian.

A pastor friend worked under a superior who picked on him so much that he became frustrated and wanted to quit. The superior bore down, getting more and more picky, spreading untrue rumors about him to the boss. The superior screamed in his face continually, and criticized his every move in front of the staff. Because he was a Christian, and the job was in a police station, he was hated without a cause and no one stood up for him. Though his family needed the money, he quit, deciding that the extreme stress was not worth it. He found a wonderful new job.

Quite simply, it may not be worth it to work with a Jezebel. The bottom line in any encounter with Jezebel is to know who *you* are. Are you spineless, cringing before the force of Jezebel's intimidating personality, or are you a king and a priest, a son of the Most High?

> **But ye are a chosen generation, a ROYAL PRIESTHOOD, a holy nation, a peculiar people; that ye should show forth the praises of Him Who hath called you out of darkness into His marvelous light. (*1 Peter 2:9*)**

We have all given up in our battle against a forceful Jezebel at one time or another, and there is no condemnation in this. My prayer is that the *next* time you encounter Jezebel you will remember "*Whose*" you are!!!

> **...we are the children of God: And if children, then heirs; heirs of God and joint-heirs with Christ... (*Romans 8:16-17*)**

20

Jezebel
Consumed
With Greed

Jezebel is rapacious and does not like others controlling the money. She must keep control of it in order to abuse and misuse it. She often lavishes it on herself, while her family/church/ business suffers. Jezebel fleeces her followers. Several pastors told me about one man with a Jezebel spirit who had collected tens of thousands of dollars from their flocks, yet when these pastors had an urgent need, he pretended to be broke and unable to help.

Another pastor told me that a man with a Jezebel spirit was holding revival at their church and demanded that *all* the tithes and offerings be given to him. The two got into a heated discussion during which the Jezebel spirit in the man yelled, "The people are coming to see *me*! I'm the one bringing them in! Give me all the money! I earned it!" He was asked to leave.

> **...be no more children, tossed to and fro, carried about with every wind of doctrine, by the sleight of men, and cunning craftiness, WHEREBY THEY LIE IN WAIT TO DECIVE.** (*Ephesians 4:14*)

Jezebel lies in wait to deceive

Sometimes a Jezebel will wait a long time before showing his/her true colors. He/she will fool a lot of people until they are in his/her snare. If God's people are deep in the Word and have a close relationship with the Father, it is harder for Jezebel to deceive them. Yet, this is not protection enough. I know of a national leader who had a Jezebel stay in his home. He and his wife considered themselves highly discerning people, yet they were grossly deceived by this person.

Plead the blood over yourself and loved ones daily, and put on your armor. If sin (such as greed, pride or a controlling spirit) has access to an individual, then Jezebel, too, will be able to fool them for a season. This is not to imply that *all* those who Jezebel fools temporarily, are in sin. Rather, I wish to state unequivocally that God's people must be constantly on guard, lest the Jezebel spirit slip in unawares and set up a stronghold. Jezebel loves ignorance and innocence, but we are to be wise as serpents and harmless as doves.

> **...if thou doest not well, sin LIETH at the door. And unto thee shall be his desire, and thou shalt rule over him. (*Genesis 4:7*)**

The word LIETH (rabats) means to crouch or hide like a recumbent animal waiting to spring on its prey. Look again at Ephesians 4:14. DECEIVE (plane) means fraudulence, delusion, error, straying from orthodoxy or piety.

> **...cunning craftiness, whereby they lie in wait to DECEIVE.**

Sin is crouching at our door. The spirit of Jezebel is gone out into the world to lead her victims into false worship. She is a ravening wolf in sheep's clothing, waiting to tear apart her victim's lives, ministries, homes, churches, businesses, whole countries, and most importantly, relationship with the true and living God.

Spirit of exhibitionism

Jezebel preys on those with a tendency toward exhibitionism. It can safely be said that many (not all) Jezebels have a tendency toward the spirit of exhibitionism, though some are very secretive. Flamboyance goes with the territory. However, not all those with a spirit of exhibitionism have a Jezebel spirit. This spirit draws attention to itself, rather than to the true God. Pelvis thrusting and any other kind of exhibitionistic dancing does not belong in a worship service. People who believe they are called to be dancers are particularly vulnerable to the spirit of exhibitionism. Heart motives need to be examined by the undividual. It is very distracting to have someone dancing in the wrong spirit, especially for the men. Women with a wrong motive or spirit will defile all who are present.

Idolatry is Jezebel's trademark

A musician related to me that an evangelist with a Jezebel spirit had told her that he made millions in the world, but he was making twice as much as an evangelist. He told the musician to quit and follow his example in order to get rich. Jezebel seduces through the lusts of the flesh and eyes, the deceitfulness of riches, and the pride of life. *(1 John 2:16)* All is vanity!

For all that is in the world, the lust of the flesh, and the lust of the eyes, and the pride of life, is not of the Father, but is of the world. (*1 John 3:16*)

This is the real reason why so many Christian musicians and singers get lured into secular music. It is the true reason why so many secular musicians and singers get saved, and for a season turn their backs on the world to serve their Savior. Then Satan chokes off their finances and soon they return to the world deeply disillusioned, often broke.

And these are they which are sown among thorns; such as hear the Word, And the cares of this world, and the deceitfulness of riches, and the lusts of other things entering in, choke the Word, and it becometh unfruitful. (*Mark 4:18-19*)

Once again they are swept up in the worldly pursuit of wealth and fame. The broad highway to hell is crowded with former servants of YHWH, and the narrow road to heaven has been deserted by many who have fallen by the wayside, having had the seed of the Word fall on stony ground, where it sprang up for a season. Later, overcome by the heat of the trials of life, they turn back from following the Savior.

And these are they likewise which are sown on STONY ground; who, when they have heard the Word, IMMEDIATELY RECEIVE IT WITH

> GLADNESS; And have NO ROOT in themselves, and
> SO ENDURE BUT FOR A TIME: afterward, when af-
> fliction or persecution ariseth for the Word's sake
> IMMEDIATELY THEY ARE ARE OFFENDED.
> (*Mark 4:16-17*)

Deception has come into their hearts and they actually believe
they are doing right to return to the secular world. All the self-
righteousness and justification in the world will not save them
when they stand before the living God.

> For it is impossible for those who were once en-
> lightened, and have tasted of the heavenly gift, and were
> made partakers of the Holy Ghost, And have tasted the
> good Word of God, and the powers of the world to
> come, If they shall fall away, to renew them again unto
> repentance; seeing they crucify to themselves the Son of
> God afresh, and put him to an open shame. (*Hebrews
> 6:4-6*)

Many are the times when Steve and I struggled financially
after we left show-business. There have been numerous temptations, but we knew that returning to the old life with all its allure
and seductive riches and glories, was a death sentence for eternity,
since we *knew to do better in our hearts*.
  My heart is heavy for show-biz personalities who have one leg
in the world and one leg in the church. Lukewarm Laodiceans will
burn because they could not commit to one god or the other. Those
who have known God, yet return to the filth of the world, like a
dog to his own vomit, are among the most wretched.

> So then because thou art LUKEWARM, and
> neither cold nor hot, I will SPEW thee out of My
> mouth. Because thou sayest, I am rich, and increased
> with goods, and have need of nothing; and knowest
> not that thou art wretched, and miserable, and poor,
> and blind, and naked... (*Revelation 3:16-17*)

Show business or ministry?

Jezebel is strongly attracted to the arts. Christian musicians
who pretend to be in ministry, but are actually in show-business,

(some are deceived but most *know* the truth), often end up in sin. This may be cleverly covered up for a season, but be sure, sin will find them out. Some end up divorced, some get others pregnant, still others are in secret adulteries. The ones you've heard about are just the tip of the iceberg.

So I gave them up unto their own hearts' lust: and they walked in their own counsels. (*Psalm 81:12*)

Some so-called Christian "performers" are into drugs and gambling, etc. Some have been exposed, but most are not. My Christian band once warmed up a "big name" Christian artist who ridiculed members of the audience and was very rude to us. Another famous "Christian" band we warmed up cussed and smoked throughout the hours of set-up, then came out and put on a pious act for the audience. I once warmed up a big-name "Christian" artist who threatened and cursed me, and ranted and raved against me for praying for the sick. I could go on and on about personal experiences, but you get the picture.

If you love Me...?

And many false prophets shall arise, and shall DECEIVE many. (*Matthew 24:11*)

DECEIVE (planao) is closely related to the word in Ephesians 4:14: **...lie in wait to DECEIVE...** It means, to *seduce*, to roam or go astray from safety, truth or virtue. When we wander from God's flock and safety of the true Shepherd, we can be easily overcome by the wolf in sheep's clothing, Jezebel.

...denying ungodliness and worldly lusts, we should live soberly, righteously, and godly, in this present world. (*Titus 2:12*)

The Jezebel influence is strong on those in the arts, but if one loves God one must *keep* His commandments. It is impossible to please God without faith for true faith declares, "I don't *care* what happens, I will not turn my back on God or bow down to Satan! It doesn't matter if I'm hungry (Jesus during his temptation), or thrown into a fiery furnace (Shadrack, Meshach and Abednego), or beaten, bitten, shipwrecked, hated (Paul), or beheaded (James,

John the Baptist, Paul), or boiled in oil (John), or hung on a cross for my faith (Jesus, Peter, Andrew). I will serve the true and living God. I may be abased or I may abound, but I won't give in to the lure of the world."

The riches of this world are but a trap, set to ensnare us.

> **For the love of money is the root of all evil; which while some coveted after, they have erred (turned away) from the faith, and PIERCED THEMSELVES THROUGH with many sorrows.** *(1 Timothy 6:10)*

We PIERCE OURSELVES THROUGH when we seek after riches. A well known preacher died on the operating table when he was still a wealthy business man. He testified that Yahshua (Jesus) appeared to him. When he realized he had thrown his life away in the pursuit of riches, he repented and asked for a chance to make it right. After being revived, he immediately sold all his businesses, and answered the call to preach the gospel. Our Savior is calling all of us into a higher realm.

> **...seek ye FIRST the kingdom of God, and His righteousness; AND ALL THESE THINGS SHALL BE ADDED unto you.** *(Matthew 6:33)*

21
Jezebel: Alive and Well In the White House

Jezebel promotes porn

Jezebel is the source of obsessive sensuality, unbridled witchcraft, and hatred for authority. Much of our government and nation is now almost completely controlled by the Jezebel spirit. I believe the office of the president has been ruled by Jezebel. A man who is prisoner to Jezebel may manifest bondage to lusts of the flesh and pornography, or be unable to control his sexual passions. Some are filled with guilt and shame, while others have consciences so seared with a hot iron that they feel nothing at all.

> **Now the Spirit speaketh expressly, that in the latter times some shall depart from the faith, giving heed to SEDUCING SPIRITS, and DOCTRINES OF DEVILS; Speaking LIES IN HYPOCRISY; having their CON-SCIENCE SEARED with a hot iron...** (*1 Timothy 4:1-2*)

The porn that American people were exposed to in the media through President Clinton's affairs has defiled them, and is evidence that Jezebel has practically taken over the media. It was made possible because the people have been *lulled into slumber* and submission by the spirit of slumber.

> **...The law is not made for a righteous man, but for the lawless and disobedient, for the ungodly and for sinners, for unholy and profane...For whoremongers, (fornicators and adulterers), for them that defile them-selves with mankind (homosexuals) ...for LIARS, for**

**PERJURED PERSONS (those who lie under oath), and
if there be any other thing that is contrary (opposed) to
sound doctrine...** *(1 Timothy 1:9-10)*

Regarding President Clinton, first, we saw announcements by
Gennifer Flowers, then Paula Jones and others followed concerning the President's affairs. These people were used by Jezebel,
to widen the gap of what can be acceptably discussed in a public
forum.

**Unto the pure all things are pure: but unto them
that are defiled and unbelieving is nothing pure; but
even their mind and conscience is defiled.** *(Titus 1:15)*

Jezebel covers truth with distraction

Then came Monica Lewinsky and her graphic testimony. What
can we say when the evening news and newspapers are so blithely
explicit that children have to be sent to their rooms in order not to
be exposed to this influence.

**...Go, and tell this people, Hear ye indeed, but un-
derstand not; and see ye indeed, but PERCEIVE NOT.**
(Isaiah 6:9)

The Lewinsky investigation was *dragged out* over time to acclimate the public into accepting that kind of information as a
regular course with the evening meal. It brought a *spirit of
slumber* into the American household that distracted us from what
was *really* going on behind the scenes in our government. Many of
our soverign rights were gradually turned over to the U.N., along
with our military and our weapons. A growing number of military
bases in the USA became occupied largely by foreign troops. The
public was snoozing, blissfully unaware. Many covert government operations were transpiring right under our noses, but we
were blitzed with rag magazine type sensationalism, instead. Our
military secrets were pedaled to the highest bidders, such as
China, while in spite of gross human rights violations they were
given "most favored nation" status.

**For the LORD hath poured out upon you the spirit
of DEEP SLEEP, and HATH CLOSED YOUR EYES:
the prophets and your rulers (leaders), the seers hath he
covered.** *(Isaiah 29:10)*

America is close to judgment from God, tribulation and imminent military takeover. Our public parks and other lands are secretly being given away to pay off national debts through executive orders on a daily basis. Yet, for a long time all the American people were fed in the news was coverage of such distractions as the O.J. Simpson trial and the President's affairs. Women continued to come forward with new, even more devastating accusations, but the nation's senses were now so dulled that no one cared. A spirit of slumber dwells in our nation.

...God hath given them the SPIRIT OF SLUMBER, EYES that they should not see, and EARS that they should not hear... (*Romans 11:8*)

Jezebel counter-attacks

In order to take the heat off herself when she is under attack, Jezebel counter-attacks. A prime example: Every time President Clinton came under attack for his wrong-doing after being elected, he and his wife launched a vicious counter-attack against his accusers. Thus, we learned that some of the people who exposed *his* affairs had engaged in affairs of their *own*. This was designed to distract us from our beleaguered president. When these tactics slightly delayed, but failed to stop the impeachment proceedings, then on the very day the vote for impeachment was to have gone forth, President Clinton ordered our troops to attack Kosovo. The result: Clinton was impeached but not ousted. The congress and the people have been engulfed with apathy, desensitized and overwhelmed with lethargy. Because of threats of their own exposure through FBI documents being illegally supplied to the Clinton administration on all their opponents, the leaders have become faint-hearted.

Jezebel promotes hatred and dissatisfaction

Jezebel engenders dissatisfaction between spouses. This spirit is fiercely independent and intensely ambitious for control. Remember when the President was trying to get elected, and his wife was asked to tone herself down, wearing drab colors and not speaking as much. We were never even told she *had* a middle name, which was her maiden name before marriage. After the election, mission accomplished, *then* came the announcement that the American people were getting *two* for the price of one.

The First Lady removed her mask of submissive behavior, and began to wear bright colors, emphatically and forcefully taking control of some operations. We were immediately informed that she was to be referred to by her *middle* name (a declaration of independence and dominance), insisting that it be announced whenever she was addressed. (Jezebel seeks recognition.)

She tried to force a system of health care on the public that would have created bondage to a socialist system. Socialism seeks to control people through seizing all the operations and actions of their lives, promoting big government, binding the people and recreating them as puppets of the state. Does this sound like Jezebel? Several of the First Lady's choices for appointments, who were proponents of women's rights and lesbians, received powerful positions of influence in the White House. Hillary Rodman has begun marching proudly in gay/lesbian parades.

Jezebel's agenda—murder

The President, overcome with lust and womanizing because of being a prisoner of Jezebel, seemed helpless to stop his actions. Meanwhile, a well known, astonishingly dominant lesbian, was made Attorney General. She pushed Jezebel's agenda of abortion, and slaughter of religious people without recrimination or apology, such as the Waco tragedy, Ruby Ridge, and the Oklahoma City bombing, which was actually an elaborate cover–up of the Waco evidence. This is not an endorsement of the Branch Davidian's peculiar religious beliefs in Waco, but rather their right to practice them without being murdered.

Jezebel is never sorry! No apology ever came forth for this or for other tragedies perpetrated on the American people. When Clinton's friend, Ron Brown, Secretary of Commerce, threatened to expose some of Clinton's illegal dealings in order to protect his own hide, he was killed in a very suspicious plane crash *the very next day.* For all those who oppose Clinton, the body count is mounting.

But the fearful, and unbelieving, and the abominable, and murderers, and whoremongers, and sorcerers, and idolaters, and all liars, shall have their part in the lake which burneth with fire and brimstone: which is the second death. (*Revelation 21:8*)

Jezebel brings destruction of family and promotes homosexual agenda

As the Jezebel spirit gained influence over our government, it was behind the promoting of gay rights, women's rights and children's rights. Jezebel is the controlling influence directing the lesser demons of homosexuality and lesbianism. One of President Clinton's first acts as leader of the free world, was to pass legislation promoting gay/lesbian rights in the military and work place. His last speech at the end of 1999 to a gay/lesbian audience was to reassure them that he was behind them 100% and would continue to do everything he could to promote their agenda.

The First Lady actively promoted children's rights. This *looks* good, but the hidden agenda behind this movement is to take away *parental* rights. Jezebel seeks to destroy the family and make the children creatures of the state. President Clinton quietly accumulated dictatorial powers through signing executive orders. Here are just a few:

- Executive order 11000, signed by President Clinton states: Seizure of all American population for work forces under federal supervision, *including dividing as necessary* according to government plans.
- Executive order 11004: Seizure of all housing, land and finance authorities to establish *forced* relocation.
- Executive order 10098 - Seizure of all food supplies and resources, public and private, all farms and farm equipment.

Executive orders need no approval from congress and can be implemented at any time, especially under marshal law declared under real or deliberately manufactured crisis. Notice these orders include dividing families according to government plans.

Jezebel seeks to destroy true religion

One magazine's headline on March 5, 1997 was, "FBI Turns Aggressive On **Terror**." (29) It stated that there were at that time 857 active patriot groups in the USA. The groups were defined as militias, common-law courts, radio broadcasters, publishers, **churches**, and others who identify themselves as anti-government and who oppose the "New World Order." *When did churches become terrorist organizations?* Time to wake up, America!

When Janet Reno was interviewed on CNN Live with Larry King, she was asked who the *radical cultists* are.

She answered, "A cultist is one who has a strong belief in the Bible and the second coming of Christ, who frequently attends Bible study, who has a high level of financial giving to a Christian cause, who home schools his children, who has accumulated survival foods, who has a strong belief in the second amendment and...a strong distrust of big government." (30) Is the church of Jesus Christ the enemy now, in our once Christian nation? Abraham Lincoln declared, "To sin by silence when one should protest makes cowards of men."

Twisted goals through wicked people

Although the President's actions toward the young intern, Lewinsky, and other women was obviously chauvinistic, manipulative, ungodly, abusive and unacceptable to the stated agenda of women's rights proponents, not one voice was raised in that camp to denounce the President, as it was in the appointment of Supreme Court Justice, Clarence Thomas, who allegedly harassed another young woman, Anita Hill, in his employ. It is important to see that this man *did* get elected to the Supreme Court, and now has a strong influence on our justice system. Remember the outcry from women's groups against *him*?

It is interesting to note that during the Nixon administration, Hillary Clinton was chosen, out of many qualified people, to be the one who sat in a room for many weeks listening to the incriminating Nixon tapes. Ultimately, upon her recommendations, she became one of the main proponents who brought accusation against Nixon for impeachment. What goes around, comes around.

Jezebel creates puppets

Jezebel used our President for her own purposes and ambitions. He was her puppet. First Lady, Hillary Roddham, fiercely defended the President, and even stated that she was *proud* of him after the Lewinsky affair was admitted to. This was the Jezebel spirit speaking directly to truly listening ears. Rather than ever expressing her hurt or concern over her husband's actions, she expressed her *anger* with those who have exposed him, vowing revenge.

The Jezebel spirit causes its victims shame and guilt. Anyone recall the public repentance of the President, tears and hanging of the head? "I have sinned."

Woe unto them that call evil good, and good evil; that put darkness for light, and light for darkness; that put bitter for sweet, and sweet for bitter! Woe unto them that are wise in their own eyes, and prudent in their own sight! (*Isaiah 5:20-21*)

How about the CIA drug connection to Governor Clinton? Jezebel often makes her victims vulnerable through drug use, and if political ambitions are present, they will be susceptible to blackmail. Anyone remember Clinton's ludicrous statement, "I smoked, but I didn't inhale."

I mentioned earlier that the New World Order crowd is moving us along swiftly toward their goal of world domination by equaling the playing field. A Vice President said in a news broadcast that he thought it unfair that U.S. citizens had such cheap food and gas, while the rest of the world has higher prices. He stated that he would change this should he become President.

The Kingdom is forcefully advancing

When Christians awake and become vigilant they can forcefully advance the Kingdom of God.

...the kingdom of heaven suffereth violence, and the VIOLENT take it by FORCE. (*Matthew 11:12*)

The word FORCE, harpazo, indicates those with eagerness and zeal, not yielding to opposition of religious foes, *pressing* their way into the kingdom. The word VIOLENT means forceful or violent men. We are to be a forceful and violent people through fervent, white-hot, burning, fiery PRAYER.

A recent documentary entitled "Transformations" has dramatically demonstrated that it *is* possible to take whole cities and nations for Yahshua Messiah (Jesus Christ). In this film four modern day, demonically controlled cities are transformed by fervent prayer into worship centers where Jesus is LORD. One pastor was murdered by drug cartels, but that didn't stop the forceful advancement of YHWH's kingdom here on earth.

In the USA a man by the name of Alexander Dowie, around the turn of the twentieth century, took the wicked city of Chicago for Jesus. Though persecuted by the police, and harassed by frequent arrests, even while hated by the post office, newspapers, crime lords, and religious groups, he stood victorious. His enemies ended up in prison, silent or dead. The police became his friends and the political officials and Mayer were voted in by Dowie's godly people. Divine healing and salvation were ultimately preached on every street corner. There is a price to pay, but the souls won for our heavenly Father are worth it.

Samson, a type of the Laodicean church, slumbered on Delilah's knees as today's church slumbers: Willful, sinful, betrayed from within, strength cut off, lacking the desire to seek God's will through prayer. He sacrificed the anointing for brief and forbidden pleasures of the flesh, blinded by the deception of carnal desire long before he was blinded literally. Yet something radically changed in his heart. When he realized his true state (wretched, blind, poor and helpless) he turned and "prayed," receiving victory that exceeded all the rest of his exploits.

Like Samson, when people run after other gods, it is because they are desperately trying to fill the emptiness in their souls. Only Jesus can fill this void! There is no other act, possession, or religion that can take His place, or satisfy their longing. If the people of America will turn their hearts toward YHWH, repent of their wicked ways and adulteries, and let the Holy Spirit lead them and guide them into all truth, He will again embrace them, and save them in the day of trouble.

If My people, which are called by My Name, shall humble themselves, and pray, and seek My face, and turn from their wicked ways; then will I hear from heaven, and will forgive their sin, and will heal their land. *(2 Chronicles 7:14)*

22

Parallels To Ancient Rome and Israel

The rise of proud, ancient Rome parallels the rise of the USA in many ways. Rome was symbolized by the eagle, had a republic and was governed by a senate. Rome went from a democratic republic to a fascist state of tyranny.

This same fate awaits America as she is overcome by the New World Order, currently being referred to as Globalism or the One World Movement. God's world is now viewed as a "global village." That village and its chiefs want to dictate how you raise your children. "It takes a whole village to raise a child," quip the patronizing leaders of this country, who insist they know more than you do about how your children should be raised.

Rome fell from within, as will America, due to the immorality of the leadership and people. The Roman people ultimately lost their freedom to despotic rulers. (31) As the moral fiber of the nation decayed into excessive decadence and they crumbled from within, they fell prey to invading hoards who destroyed them from without. Would it surprise you to learn that this same fate has been planned for the United States?

> **For, behold, the day cometh, that shall burn as an oven; and all the proud, yea, and all that do wickedly, shall be stubble: and the day that cometh shall burn them up, saith the LORD of hosts, that it shall leave them neither root nor branch. But unto you that fear My Name shall the Sun of righteousness arise with healing in His wings...** (*Malachi 4:1-2*)

Israel was destroyed as a nation during the reign of her 42nd king. William Jefferson Clinton is the United States of America's 42nd President, and Queen Elizabeth is the 42nd monarch to rule Great Britain. (32) The extention we are being given (Bush) shows that YHWH's people are praying.

> **Thus saith the Lord God; It shall also come to pass,
> that at the same time shall things come into thy mind,
> and thou shall think an evil thought: And thou shalt
> say, I will go up to them that are at rest, that dwell
> safely, all of them dwelling without walls, and
> having neither bars nor gates, to take a spoil, and to
> take a prey; to turn thine hand upon the desolate places
> that are now inhabited, and upon the people that are
> gathered out of the nations which have gotten cattle and
> goods, that dwell in the midst of the land. (*Ezekiel
> 38:10-12*)**

On a recent special broadcast entitled "Hitler and the Holy
Grail," it was revealed that Himmler (head of the SS) believed he
was living in the final era of the disintegration of Christianity. He
set out to eliminate it from German life. Gabriele Winkler, from
Himmler's personal staff, stated, "We had been **smothered** by the
Christian/Judaic religion. We wanted to revive the traditions that
appealed to us."

Himmler created a new religion that was a curious blend of
medieval myth, Nordic legend and pure fakery, much like the
Romans exhibited in their hodge podge pantheon of gods.
Germans were determined to turn their backs on what they considered to be repression by tradional religious beliefs. Florentine
Rost van Tonningen, widow of a senior SS officer, said, "Himmler
was a man of vision...You could compare the war to a holy
war...Our philosophy was so noble...There is no purer, more
intense, and intellectually higher body than the SS."

> **Then shall they deliver you up to be afflicted, and
> shall kill you: and ye shall be hated of all nations for
> My Name's sake. And then shall MANY be offended,
> and shall betray one another: and shall hate one
> another. (*Matthew 24:9-10*)**

The word MANY in this verse means *majority*. One day soon
the sleeping church will awaken and it will be too late.
Persecution and tribulation will begin and many true believers will
be slaughtered. Our only hope is in *total* surrender to YHWH
with heartfelt repentance, humbling ourselves under the mighty
hand of our God.

The prophet Jonah was sent to an appallingly wicked city
called Nineveh. Amazingly, when he preached their destruction,

they all repented. The Ninevites were a cruel, Baal worshiping people who disemboweled enemies while still alive, cut off their heads and threw them in a pile at the gate of the city. They were feared and hated throughout the known world, yet these heathen people repented.

> **Behold, I stand at the DOOR, and knock: if any man hear My voice, and open the door, I will come in to him, and will sup with him, and he with Me.** (*Revelation 3:20*)

The DOOR is the human heart and it can only be opened from the inside. Jesus wept when everyone else was rejoicing at His triumphant entrance into Jerusalem because the people didn't know *the time of their visitation*. I pray this would not happen to America. I pray for revival which can only begin with heartfelt repentance.

> **And when He was come near, He beheld the city, and WEPT over it, Saying, If thou hadst known, even thou, at least in this thy day, the things which belong unto thy peace! but now they are HID FROM THINE EYES. For the days shall come upon thee, that thine enemies shall cast a trench about thee, and compass thee round, and keep thee in on every side, And shall lay thee even with the ground, and thy children within thee; and they shall not leave in thee one stone upon another; BECAUSE THOU KNEWEST NOT THE TIME OF THY VISITATION.** (*Luke 19:41-44*)

Will we miss Yahshua the Messiah again? Will we turn our backs on His tender mercies while they are still extended to us, or will we wait until the door to the wedding supper has been closed and it is too late?

> **And the foolish said to the wise, Give us of your oil; for our lamps are gone out....And while they went to buy, the bridegroom came; and THEY THAT WERE READY WENT IN with him to the marriage: and the DOOR WAS SHUT.** (*Matthew 25:8, 10*)

23

The god of Self: Abortion and the Hardened Heart

Because of pride and arrogance, Jezebel leads nations in idolatry, so that they refuse to yield to the one true God. She promotes her own brand of religion: the religion of *self*. It has been the downfall of every great nation. Remember the earlier quote from Gabriele Winkler, stating that the Nazis wished to create a new religion, free of supposed repression, with traditions that "appealed to them." Himmler's plan was to foment extreme national PRIDE for which the people would be willing to fight and die.

We have heard of the PRIDE of Moab; he is very proud: even of his haughtiness, and his pride, and his wrath. But his lies shall not be so. (*Isaiah 16:6*)

America has sinned in her pride and arrogance just as the Romans, the Germans and Moab did. She has thumbed her nose at holiness, truth and righteousness. She has failed to protect the defenseless; 45 million slaughtered unborn through abortion.

If thou FORBEAR to deliver them that are drawn unto death, and those that are ready to be slain; if thou sayest, Behold, we knew it not; doth not He that pondereth the heart consider it? (*Proverbs 24:11-12*)

The word FORBEAR, chasak, means refrain, refuse, hinder, hold back, withhold. We have refused, held back, even hindered saving the helpless unborn. Their blood is crying out from the ground as Abel's blood did. Our President refused to sign the bill that Congress worked hard to pass banning partial birth abortions. If he was ever going to make a move to do something morally right, this was his big chance, with all of Congress and the nation behind it, but he dropped the ball, just as Ahab dropped the ball after the victory on Mount Carmel.

Once Israel was opened up to Baal worship, they also began to worship Molech, the national god of Ammon. (33) Molech's followers caused their children to pass through the fire. Fire built under the stone hands of Molech's statue, made the hands red-hot. The people sacrificed their firstborn infants on these hands. As they burned alive, their screams were ignored, but YHWH heard, just as He hears the cries of the millions of aborted babies today.

> **...when ye make prayers, I will not hear: your hands are full of blood...** (*Isaiah 1:15*)

In an article from *Creators Syndicate*, a medical technician, working for a firm that trafficked in baby parts, gives some shocking information. She dissected the aborted fetuses in order to obtain "high-quality" parts for sale: Eyes and ears go for $75, brains for $999, intact trunks fetch $500, a whole liver $150. One day a set of twins at 24 weeks gestation were brought to her in a pan. They were both alive. The doctor said: "Got you some good specimens—twins." She looked at him and said, "There's something wrong here. They are moving. I can't do this. This in not in my contract." He took a bottle of water and poured it until it covered their mouths and noses and drowned them.

She said whenever there were live births, the doctor would either break the neck or take a pair of tongs and beat the baby until it was dead. Sometimes the fetus would appear to be dead, but when the chest was opened up, the heart was still beating. Sometimes the type of abortion was altered in order to produce better tissue for selling later.

Abortion clinics team up with body part's brokers sharing space and costs right in the same clinic, reducing human beings to the level of mere commodities. One body parts company, Opening Lines Inc., advertises, "The highest quality, most affordable, freshest tissue prepared to your specifications and delivered in the quantities you need, when you need it." What difference is there between sacrificing infants to Molech and Baal, and in sacrificing fetuses to the god of selfishness and greed, openly trafficking in body parts.

Get them while they're young—and they can't depart

Satan uses Jezebelian mothers (and fathers) to target children. It is no accident that many talented people have a parent who is excessively critical, domineering or overbearing. This creates insecure, unhappy children who obsessively seek the approval of others. They become vulnerable as man pleasers and man's prophets, rather than God pleasers and God's prophets. Satan's intent is to pervert the gifts of God from an early age for his own use. Thus, many gifted people gravitate toward acceptance via performance, rather than turning toward the living God to receive His love freely. Performance oriented people have trouble accepting that there is nothing they can ever do to earn God's love and His salvation, the good news that is a free gift.

Whether the child becomes homosexual or not, he or she will be, at the very least, extremely insecure, seeking show-business or some other flamboyant career to boost self-image. The parent may actually push the child in this direction to bolster his or her own ego, becoming relentless, pushy, never satisfied, forever critical and very controlling. The child may become an over or under-achiever, anorexic or bulimic, emotionally wounded, withdrawn, rebellious or a victimizer, in turn.

Because the sins of the parents *do* come down on the child, generational curses must be broken. Bitter-root judgments and inner vows must be broken, too, along with unhealthy soul ties. (Get my book or teaching tape on these subjects for a step-by-step explanation on how to be set free.) All of us have known people who are overly attached to, or wounded by a parent, seemingly under their control even years after they leave home.

It takes inner healing to set such a captive free. Rejection, self-pity, depression, poor self-image, a spirit of heaviness, suicide, and possibly the same spirits that work through Jezebel must be cast out of the victim of a Jezebelian parent. Because of judgments and offenses they have sown against their parents, they themselves will reap back, multiplied many times, what they have sown. This victim must have forgiveness at the top of the list in order to be set free.

24

Exposing Pokemon and Other Games

Jezebel is after the children

When a friend of mine returned from a flight to California, she related that she was seated with a girl and boy, seven and nine years old, traveling alone. All they talked about was witches and vampires. She tried several times to change the subject, but they chattered incessantly about their idols from TV.

I told her that with all the TV shows like "Sabrina, Teenage Witch," "Buffy, the Vampire Slayer," (both full of graphic demonstrations of the occult and witchcraft) and most of the cartoons and video games, how can we expect our children not to be heavily influenced. We've come a long way since "Bewitched." If parents will not monitor their children's viewing time, then the children will be overcome with unnatural curiosity and obsession with the occult. The lust for power obtained through the occult is a natural progression of events.

Gotta' catch them all

The occult can come through seemingly innocent games such as Pokemon, which, according to their own promo is short for pocket-monster. The obsession begins with the theme song which repeats over and over like a *mantra*, "Gotta catch 'em, gotta catch 'em *all!*" The children repeat and sing this song, unknowingly participating in a form of enchantment which is used in New Age religions, Hinduism, Masonry, witchcraft, etc. These mind-numbing exercises open the mind up to invasion from demons. There are over 150 Pokemon, and children know them all by name. The game becomes an addiction which captures the minds of our children with chilling efficiency. (34)

Wizards of the Coast—Dungeons and Dragons

Dungeons and Dragons is put out by a company that call themselves Wizards of the Coast (wizards are male practitioners of black magic). One of their subsidiaries, known as T.S.R., produces "Dungeons and Dragons," a demonic and highly addictive role playing game. Numerous teenage suicides are linked to this game. (35)

Magic—the Gathering

Another particularly demonic game, produced by the same company, is called "Magic—the Gathering," a self-described occult game of the same genre. In this game, players can "summon" spirits at will and some children have been known to order them, "Enter me!" A sampling of cards that come with the game are: Necromancer (a medium who talks with the dead; strictly forbidden in scripture); All Hallows Eve; Sorcery, which means witchcraft via drugs (on this card appears a demon, a carved pumpkin, a black cat, and a full moon). Instructions are to summon spirits from the graveyard to do the bidding of the player. Another card, Magician, shows a magician kneeling with demons on either side. These two games constitute specific "how-to manuals" in the art of witchcraft. They include actual spells and formulas, taken directly from books on witchcraft, incantations and role-playing. (36)

Pokemon

Pokemon is another game manufactured by Wizards of the Coast. It is no accident, regardless of how innocent Pokemon appears at the outset, that the symbols and characters of Pokemon reflect their creator's field of expertise, the occult. It is established through the other games they have manufactured that the people who produce Pokemon are knowledgeable in the Satanic arts. As pictured in the *Pokemon Players Guide*, the "energy" balls the Pokemon use to launch attacks (energy is a New Age expression for demonic presence) clearly carry known symbols of witchcraft, Satanism and New Age religions. (37) One example is the electric lightening bolt or satanic "S", which was also incorporated by the Nazis in their "SS" symbol. Hitler was an avid believer and user of black magic. The symbol of a LIGHTNING bolt to represent Satan originates from these references to Satan's fall from heaven, found in the scriptures. Satan has certainly succeeded in WEAKENING the children through this game.

And He (Jesus) said unto them, I beheld Satan as LIGHTNING fall from heaven. *(Luke 10:18)*

How art thou FALLEN FROM HEAVEN, O Lucifer, son of the morning! how are thou cut down to the ground, which didst WEAKEN THE NATIONS! *(Isaiah 14:12)*

Another "energy" symbol in Pokemon is the "all seeing eye," symbol of the third eye in Hinduism, occultism, witchcraft, Masonry and New Age religions that practice Transcendental Meditation. (38) Dark Golduck, a Pokemon, has a jewel in the middle of its forehead which is a third eye, by which it evokes psychic powers. There are several other Pokemon that have a third eye.

A third "energy" symbol is the "clenched fist." (39) The clenched fist stands for rebellion or revolution. Three other Pokemon "energies" which are powerful symbols of the basic elements in witchcraft are "earth" (also a new age symbol), "water" (which translates into wind) and "fire." They are also symbolized by an upside down triangle. There are other energies, but according to the *Pokemon Players Guide*, these supernatural energy balls are used to make the Pokemon bigger and better monsters. (40) Ask yourself whether these symbols were put in Pokemon by coincidence, or whether they were strategically placed in Pokemon to acclimate and desensitize our children to the occult?

The guide also states that the object is to catch *all* the Pokemon, thereby becoming a Pokemon Master. What child would not jump at the chance to be a "master?" Children are led by the guide to believe that they can call on the powers that are in the cards. An incident that made headlines in Montreal detailed a boy getting stabbed with a four inch knife while trying to reclaim his brother's Pokemon cards. (41)

The Pokemon players are constantly told, "You have the power at your fingertips!" Another sobering incident occurred in Lakeland, Florida, where a teacher was hit in the face for confiscating a disruptive student's Pokemon cards. The child told his parents, "They were trying to steal my powers!" (42)

One of the cutest Pokemon characters, Pikachu, has a tail in the shape of a **lightening** bolt (Who is it that fell as **lightening** from heaven?). Another character, Mewtwo, is a very dark, foreboding character, appearing like an alien or demon, and always has his left hand in the "hail Satan" configuration. (43) Three other characters, Poliwhirl, Poliwag and Poliwrath have the swirling symbol of hypnotism on their chests. The spiral is a symbol in witchcraft for male fertility, and is used to mesmerize its victims in Pokemon. (44) Another Pokemon named Drowzee is a character that evolves into a Pokemon named Hypno. Hypno carries a special pendant for hypnotizing that emits sleep waves.

An especially satanic character is Alakazam. It is configured to look like the goat-headed, five-pointed star, Baphomet, symbolic of Satan, a powerful symbol in witchcraft. Alakazam uses a confusion ray and super-intelligence to defeat enemies. Two additional characters are Abra and Kadabra. Together, these two words form the basis of a magic spell. Abra uses its ability to read minds to detect danger and teleport (astro-travel) to safety. Additionally, it operates in telekinesis (moving objects with the mind—this is really done by demons). Kadabra has a pentagram on its forehead and the three satanic "SSS's," lightening bolts, across its chest. This symbol means "Satan's Solemn Servant." Kadabra is always pictured with its left hand giving the satanic salute. (45) All three of these characters use psychic powers. Kadabra and Alakazam both bend spoons with their minds according to the official handbook.

Weepingbell, a frightful character, uses a razor-leaf attack, spits out poison power to immobilize its enemies and finishes them with a spray of acid. Nice images for our children! Jynx is a Pokemon that meditates and is psychic. It wiggles its enchanting hips and uses a kissing technique to put its opponents to sleep.

Other Pokemon, according to *The Official Pokemon Handbook*, Gastly, Haunter and Gengar, a trio of poisonous, ghost Pokemon, are very sinister, scary images. They use hypnosis to put their victims to sleep, then become dream-eaters who attack other Pokemon while sleeping. There have been numerous reports of children having nightmares in which these characters appeared. (46) The demons, invited in to play with the children during waking hours, feel free to attack them in their dreams.

Sabrina, a human character, is a psychic gym leader using only psychic Pokemon to battle with. She trains people to use psychic powers, such as spoon bending and psychic card reading. Her eyes are like cat slits that light up. She uses a doll which she controls with her mind according to the official handbook.

Koffing, another Pokemon, has a skull and cross-bones high-lighted on its belly with a sick smile on its hideously swollen, red lips. It poisons and confuses its victims and is prone to exploding, according to the collectible Pokemon cards.

Doom and Quake

Two computer and video games, "Doom" and "Quake," have been cited as strong factors in the Paduca, Kentucky slayings of eight school children and the massacre of twelve high school students and one teacher at Columbine High School in Littleton, Colorado. The killers were known to be avid players of these video and computer games, which teach players how to shoot and murder others, even allowing the player to superimpose the face of intended victims on the screen, as was done in the above cases. A quote from the game Quake states, "They made up a god and called him Christianity. Your God is dead and no one cares!" (47) The manufacturer of the games claims *no* responsibility in the current law suits against them.

Resident Evil

Another popular game, called "Resident Evil," features flesh-eating zombies who in graphic 3-D chase and continually grab and kill the players, who can watch while their own flesh is torn off the bone. These zombies must be shot in the head to be stopped. (48)

Harry Potter

The astonishing success of this series of books is not so sur-prising, after all. The books are loaded with witchcraft, magic spells and are really a how-to guide into the occult. They stimulate cu-riosity and fascination with the occult in young and old alike.

Furby

Another popular toy for children is the furry creature, Furby, which possesses a very high-tech computer chip that learns and develops language at an amazing rate. They look like Gremlins. Unfortunately, the creatures already have names identical to those of demons and Celtic gods. In other words, the toy becomes a conduit into your home for demons. In one instance, a Christian man removed the batteries, and though impossible in the natural, the doll continued to make angry noises and said to him, "I don't like you." When the demon was cast out of the doll by name, the doll became silent. The owners burned it. (49)

Satanic rock group

When I was in the world, before being born again, I went with the leader of a famous satanic rock group. One of their songs led several teenagers across the nation to commit suicide. I used to sit on top of an amplifier behind the musicians, and observe the laser light show that destroyed the retinas of their fan's eyes. I asked the leader how he wrote the songs for his albums and he related that they would all get in a room and the songs would come by automatic writing. Then they would send the master tape to a witch coven to be prayed over before the records were pressed, so that demons would go home with every album. This is a common practice both here and amongst some foreign manufacturers of various products.

Battleground for the mind

The battle is for the minds of our children. The devil wants to *"catch them all"* while they are young and indoctrinate them with symbols and knowledge from satanic sources, all the while dressing it up as cute, and not so cute games, TV programs and music that are actually steps toward the occult designed to bypass the child's sense of right and wrong, and create obsessive behavior.

The children are lulled into a state of slumber and desensitized to violence through repeated exposure to these ungodly materials. This is, quite simply, part of the master plan of Jezebel and we have been her willing puppets.

25

Jezebel's Predecessors and Successors

Delilah—-temptress and seductress

Delilah was a type and shadow of Jezebel. She brought down, through her lustful seductions, the celebrated judge of Israel, Samson. *(Judges 16:4-31)* Through her forceful persistence, she succeeded in luring Samson into betraying his people; Jezebel succeeded in luring Ahab to betray the Israelites.

Delilah perished in a snare of her own making with 3,000 Philistines, foolishly underestimating the power of Samson's God, just as Jezebel miscalculated the power of Elijah's God. Delilah did not repent, but was in the temple to mock Samson and YHWH when she was smashed beneath the pillars, still defiant and unrepentant. Jezebel too, was smashed and trampled on the ground for defying YHWH. It is not wise to mock, challenge or oppose the God Who created you, yet that is exactly what these two women did.

Be not deceived; God is not MOCKED: for whatsoever a man soweth, that shall he also reap. (*Galatians 6:7*)

Samson sinned by taking a wife who worshipped a pagan god, just as Ahab did by marrying the heathen, Jezebel. Samson had power as long as he kept his vow to God not to cut his hair or tell anyone the source of his strength. The *real* strength behind any man of God is YHWH, Himself.

Imagine sacrificing all of mankind for one luscious taste of fruit. Adam's power was cut off and a curse came on him when he allowed himself to be seduced into tasting the forbidden fruit in Eden. Samson's power was taken from him when he yielded to the wily seducer, Delilah. She was a tantalizing Philistine tidbit, a moment's forbidden pleasure. Though he was celebrated for his acts of strength and fearlessness, he melted in defeat at Delilah's knees. Likewise, Ahab lost his power through weakness and lust when he allowed Jezebel to take over the leadership of Israel for a few grapes in a forbidden vineyard.

As Delilah seduced Samson and cut off his power, so Jezebel seduced Ahab and cut off the source of his power: YHWH's leadership through the king. Delilah severed Samson of his manhood and leadership for filthy lucre, while lulling him to sleep on her knees. Jezebel destroyed Naboth while lulling Ahab into a spirit of slumber, inviting him to hide in his palace, thereby removing any remaining hope for the continuation of their dynasty. Jezebel destroyed Ahab for a vineyard, and Delilah destroyed Samson for 5,500 pieces of silver. The Jezebel spirit should be depicted as a snake coiled enticingly around oversized grapes labeled: lusts of the flesh, lust of the eyes and the pride of life.

Love not the world, neither the things that are in the world. If any man love the world, the love of the Father is not in him. For all that is in the world, the LUST OF THE FLESH, and the LUST OF THE EYES, and the PRIDE OF LIFE, is not of the Father, but is of the world. And the world passeth away, and the lust thereof: but he that doeth the will of God abideth for ever. (*1 John 2:15-17*)

Jezebel generates unbelief and fear

The spirit of Elijah was placed on John the Baptist, who was again confronted by the Jezebel spirit, manifesting through Herodias. She had him killed for exposing the sin of her marriage to her brother-in-law, just as Elijah exposed the sin of Ahab's marriage to Jezebel. Herodias hated John, as Jezebel hated Elijah. Herod was a weak, vacillating king who had trouble making decisions, just as Ahab before him. They were both vulnerable to sexual seduction and temptation. Herodias' daughter, Salome, was used in a plot to destroy John the Baptist, through her "seductive dance" before Herod.

Both Herodias and Jezebel were controlling, ambitious and had weak, wicked husbands. Both tried to destroy God's prophet; Herodias succeeded. Both plotted for position and power, and both were pulled down from power in disgrace.

John became discouraged and fearful in prison and sent his disciples to inquire of Yahshua (Jesus) whether He was truly the Messiah, even though he had already witnessed to others that He was Messiah, having seen the Holy Spirit descending on Him with his own eyes. Elijah ran away in discouragement, too.

The Jezebel spirit makes men's hearts grow faint with fear and unbelief; she causes men to doubt what they know in their hearts. As doubts germinate in them they waver, even in their most well known mandates from God.

Jezebel's daughter

Athaliah, daughter of the insatiably wicked Jezebel, was even *more* wicked than her mother. She was fanatically devoted to Baalism. She was the only woman to reign as queen of Judah, but she usurped the throne illegally (sound like Jezebel?) through much bloodshed. She was given in marriage to Jehoram who reigned for eight years. Though Jehoram came from a godly heritage, evil relationships do corrupt good morals. *(1 Corinthians 15:33)* He made himself part of the house of Ahab, as did his son, Ahaziah, by yielding to sin. They both allowed Jezebel's influence to prevail and in the end were all destroyed because of it.

And he (Jehoram) WALKED IN THE WAY OF THE KINGS OF ISRAEL, like as did the house of Ahab: FOR HE HAD THE DAUGHTER OF AHAB TO WIFE: and he wrought that which was evil in the eyes of the LORD. *(2 Chronicles 21:6)*

Jehoram was under the same black magic spell that Ahab had languished under: the evil witchcraft of Baal worshippers. This is why the LORD commands us not to be unequally yoked with unbelievers through marriage. *(2 Corinthians 6:14)* Athaliah dominated him as her mother had dominated Ahab, tyrannically introducing Baal worship to Judah (as her mother had done to Israel) and partially tearing down YHWH's temple, to use some of these materials in building Baal's temple.

Corrupt fruit from a corrupt tree

Athaliah's son, Ahaziah, reigned for only one year. The Bible
relates that he was a wicked king, *following the forceful counsel
of his mother*. Evil continued to permeate this line of Baal worshippers, generation after generation.

> **He also walked in the ways of the house of Ahab:
> FOR HIS MOTHER WAS HIS COUNSELOR TO DO
> WICKEDLY. Wherefore he did evil in the sight of the
> LORD like the house of Ahab: for they were his coun-
> selors after the death of his father to his destruction.**
> (*2 Chronicles 22:3-4*)

Athaliah was a queen for eight years, a queen mother for one
year and she ruled alone for six years. She seized the throne by
massacring all her grandchildren except one, Joash, who was
hidden away for the six years of her reign. On the day he was
coronated in the temple, she burst in shouting, "Treason!" The
worst offender yet, she screamed the loudest. She was slain
without pity as her mother before her, and died as she had lived:
violently. She was thrown into the horse path, where she was
trampled as her mother had been, destroyed by her own
wickedness.

> **Then Jehoiada the priest...said unto them...
> WHOSO FOLLOWETH HER, LET HIM BE SLAIN
> WITH THE SWORD. For the priest said, Slay her
> not in the house of the LORD. So they laid hands on
> her; and when she was come to the entering of the
> horse gate by the king's house, they slew her there.**
> (*2 Chronicles 23:14-15*)

The priest did not want her blood to defile the house of
YHWH, so she was taken to the horse gate to be slain. She
perished a queen, granddaughter, daughter, wife, mother and
grandmother of kings, yet in her death she was in the gall of bitterness, without a queen's burial (like mother, like daughter) or a
single person to mourn her passing. The law of sowing and
reaping had increased in its yield of wickedness through Athaliah.

> **For they have sown the wind, and they shall reap the whirlwind...** *(Hosea 8:7)*

A chilling note accompanies her death warrant: Who ever chooses to follow her in her evil, idolatrous ways, will be slain with the sword. This *same* threat is sealed in the passage of Revelation 2:22-23, concerning Jezebel.

> **Behold, I will cast her into a bed, and THEM THAT COMMIT ADULTERY WITH HER INTO GREAT TRIBULATION, except they repent of their deeds. And I WILL KILL HER CHILDREN WITH DEATH...**

The Jezebel spirit lived big in Athaliah. Her life mirrored her mother's as did her death. Jezebel has had many "daughters" since Athaliah's death. Ungodly parents who have done wickedly will produce children who will be as bad or worse than they are. God cannot be mocked. As they sow, so shall they reap. Ahab's father was wicked. Jezebel's father killed his own brother to become king and was a wicked high priest of Baal. Just look at their tainted bloodlines. YHWH had to wipe them out to salvage anything of the two kingdoms, Israel and Judah.

Note: The same hot-tempered bloodline Jezebel sprang from, produced the despotic conqueror, Hannibal, who also shared her bad temperament. (50)

26

The Blessing or Curse of Identity

Generational blessing and generational cursing are often overlooked when we try to understand why some people come readily to the cross and receive salvation, while others, no matter what you say or do, simply refuse to hear the good news. An important part of our identity is our bloodline.

First we will take a look at a man named Max Jukes, who lived 200 years ago. Max was an atheist who married a godless woman. Together they had 560 descendants. Out of this number:

310 died paupers
150 became criminals
7   were murderers
100 were known drunkards
    more than half of the women were prostitutes

Max Jukes' descendants cost the U.S. government more than 1.25 million dollars in 19th century dollars, the equivalent of 15 million dollars today. (51)

Jonathan Edwards, on the other hand, was a contemporary of Max Jukes, and a very well known preacher. He played a key role in the Great Awakening. He entered Yale at age thirteen and in 1727 he became an associate pastor of his *"grandfather's"* church in Massachusetts. Two years later he became the pastor. He preached what is probably the best known revival sermon of all time, "Sinners in the Hands of an Angry God." He served as a missionary to the Indians and became president of what was later called Princeton University. (52)

Jonathan Edwards put God first place in his life, was a committed Christian and he married a godly wife. He had 1,394 descendants that were traced; almost three times as many as Max. Out of this number:

295 graduated college
13   were college presidents
65   were professors
3   were U.S. Senators
3   were State Governors
30   were judges
100 were lawyers
1   Dean of an outstanding law school
56   practiced as physicians
1   Dean of medical school
75   were officers in the military
80   held public office
3   were Mayors of large cities
1   was comptroller of the U.S. Treasury
1   was Vice President of the United States
100 were well known missionaries, preachers and
     prominent authors
Others: ministers of the government to foreign countries (53)

Not one of Jonathan Edwards' descendants was a liability to the U.S. government. They were productive citizens. This constitutes a graphic demonstration of a blessed heritage versus a cursed heritage. Notice that Jonathan's grandfather was a pastor and a number of his descendants went into ministry.

If you have been born again, you become a descendent of the "first born from the dead," Jesus. If you continue to live a godly life, then your descendants have a godly impartation that will continue to escalate in blessings.

Max Jukes had an impartation from his father, the devil, that poisoned his bloodline with addictions, strife, sin, etc. This became a devastating cycle of hurts and wounds, unforgiveness, bitterness, hatred, murder, witchcraft, whoredoms, etc.

Often, if I'm ministering to someone who is having a difficult time receiving ministry or deliverance, I will sit them down and begin asking about their parents, grandparents, and great-great grandparents. Almost without exception, information relevant to the current crisis will be revealed. If the person is suffering from addiction to anything, such as bouts of rage or sexual sin, I can almost guarantee that Grandpa or Dad or someone in their bloodline had the same demonic strongholds in their lives. Generational curses must be broken.

Recently, I was doing some business when a friend's sister showed up. She was despondent and burst into tears. I canceled the rest of the day's business to minister to her. Everything in her life had become a cycle of failure: divorce, personal illness, a son in rebellion with A.D.D., depression, and she had recently lost her job. Self-image was at an all-time low.

Through a word of knowledge, I began to ask her about her father and some early childhood abuse. She had been molested by him and others, married early to get away and failed miserably at just about everything. Her father, grandfather, brother and other relatives had been alcoholics, drug addicts, abusers, molesters, shown no love, and had been poor providers. Her father died of sclerosis of the liver.

First, I broke generational curses. Then we began a time of deep repentance. She had a hard time forgiving her father and I knew that this was the key to her breakthrough. I have found that this is often the case, but I told her that her forgiveness gets *her* off the hook with God and produces a clean heart in her. Then God can deal with her offenders. I cast out several demons and then we worked together to break some bitter-root judgments, soul ties and inner vows. (Get my tape or book on these subjects.)

I led her to the LORD and we began a time of instruction in the Word. Afterward, she took my book *Stripes, Nails, Thorns and The Blood* on spiritual warfare, deliverance and healing. She called me two weeks later to let me know that she was doing great, feeling better and had a job. What a difference the *blessing* of the LORD can make in a life.

Max Jukes must have heard of God, for he lived in the time of the Great Awakening when thousands were turning their lives around, yet the record reveals that he stubbornly held to atheism. Conversely, if someone's life seems blessed and their family serves Jesus, often the blessings of a godly heritage will play a major role. This compelling study of two very different American families, who were contemporaries of one another, reveals just how important godly heritage can be.

Jezebel came from a cursed bloodline. Ahab also had a cursed bloodline. Their descendants were cursed as well, and in the end they were all cut off because of turning their backs on the true and living God, YHWH. God's mercy was available, but as we have seen, they repeatedly refused to take it.

27

Distinguishing Between the Controlling Spirit and the Jezebel Spirit

The difference between the controlling spirit and the Jezebel spirit is not to be taken lightly. There are many people running around accusing others of having a Jezebel spirit when the accused person really has a controlling spirit. Falsely accusing people we feel threatened by is inappropriate. One must be careful not to start slinging names around. Just because someone has a forceful personality does not mean she/he has a Jezebel spirit, however both the controlling and the Jezebel spirit operate through witchcraft.

Examples—people who manifest controlling spirits

One example of a pastor with a controlling spirit is the shepherd who is fearful of losing "his" flock to some other church, and constantly preaches against other churches. Other examples are pastors or leaders who *order* their flocks or followings not go to meetings at some other place or church; leaders who hound their congregations about tithing in order to manipulate the people into giving beyond their means; pastors who are fearful of people's liberty in Yahshua Messiah (Jesus Christ). The fear is that they might get into sin without a constant emphasis on sin; this is lack of faith in the Holy Spirit's ability to lead men to repentance, therefore they constantly preach on sin, sin, sin, to awake a sin consciousness in the congregation, rather than a more balanced message that includes God's mercy.

Husbands or wives with controlling spirits often demand to
have an accounting of every penny spent and oppress their
families under extreme strictness and rigidity. A spouse cannot
leave the house without being grilled about her/his every move.
Often a spirit of jealousy, division and strife will accompany the
controlling spirit. The controller may exhibit anger if the spouse
is gone too long. Fear may enter into the oppressed spouse, or mo-
tivate the controller into jealousy. (Wives, there is a *difference*
between godly submission to your *husband* and submitting to a
demon.) Controllers aren't willing to serve, but desire others to
serve them. This is not God's way.

Humility is the key to great leadership. One who yells and
demands that others submit, is not leading according to biblical
standards. Following someone who manifests this behavior is, in
reality, following a demon who is using the person. People under
this kind of leadership may be stressed, fearful and deeply
wounded. The likelihood that they will take up offenses and be
bitter is very high. Conversely, people under godly leadership will
be blessed and honored to follow, not to mention willing.

**...whosoever will be chief among you, let him be
your SERVANT.** (*Matthew 20:25*)

The controller may operate with a religious spirit that engenders extreme fanaticism. Rigid or finicky demands on
housekeeping are common. Harsh treatment of the children is
often the case. The tyrannical church leader is often extreme in
rejection of other leaders or churches. Those who follow them
must exhibit their same views or be fired. They will usually be
hard to work with, demanding and unreasonable on certain issues.
The controller will have a high turnover in personnel on the job
and in the church. The controller may manipulate by yelling,
pouting, threatening physically, emotionally or through exposure
of deeds, cursing, posture or exhibitionism. These are forms of
witchcraft. The controller may even pray controlling prayers or
witchcraft prayers.

 Often, the person with a controlling spirit is motivated by fear.
If they let go, they fear chaos, and suffer from lack of trust in God
to perform His Word. Therefore, the controller suffers from *doubt*
and *unbelief* in religious and personal matters. The pastor with a
controlling spirit is afraid the people won't give enough, or afraid
they might run off to another church and stay.

The controlling pastor or leader is not trusting God to meet his needs, so he resorts to manipulation and witchcraft to control the people. I know of one church that has the people recite outloud their creed every Sunday. Included in this litany is a vow to give and tithe, and be loyal to *that* church. The sheep don't realize they are being compelled, controlled and manipulated by these ungodly vows.

At one church, a family had just purchased a beautiful van. When the pastor saw it in the parking lot he remarked loudly that he'd had a dream in which God had given him a van exactly like it, and how much he needed a new van. The family felt guilty for having a new van, and under pressure, gave the pastor their new van. He bragged continually about the new van *God* gave him, but everyone knew he had gotten it with his own manipulations.

A person with a controlling spirit can, and sometimes does, repent. One pastor at a large church repented publicly after attending a revival. He was deeply convicted of controlling and manipulating the flock, and of his own fear of revival. He secretly thought the people would get wild and he would lose control. Instead, the whole church went into several months of revival, with much weeping, repenting, worship and renewal.

Jezebel, on the other hand, manifests in a much deeper apostasy. She promotes deviation from the truth of the gospel. She uses and destroys the saints and prophets in order to accomplish her agenda: To turn the people's hearts away from the true God. She is vengeful and wanton in her pursuit of power and lusts of the flesh. She is a master deceiver.

In a nutshell, a person with a controlling spirit *can* be brought to repentance, but Jezebel never repented; people with Jezebel spirits rarely repent. If you believe you or someone you know has a controlling spirit, follow the steps below.

Steps for repentance from a controlling spirit

1. If you have used control, which is really witchcraft, to manipulate others, regardless of whether the motivation for your actions is from fear or ignorance, ***repent!***
2. Ask for God's forgiveness and mercy.
3. Cast out the controlling spirit and resist the temptation to take it up again.

4. Cast out a spirit of fear, deception, witchcraft, murder (if there has been anger or violence), and any other spirit that is operating and manifesting.

5. Ask the Holy Spirit to reveal areas where you are operating in this wicked spirit. Pray for strength, guidance and wisdom to stop this behavior.

6. Learn to hate this sin and the behaviors that go with it.

7. Some controlling behaviors include, but are not limited to: whining, complaining, anger, violence, suspiciousness, playing sick, demanding, shouting, cursing, lying, pouting, slamming things, murmuring, threatening, stubbornness, loud talking, manipulation, micro-managing, inability to delegate, selfishness, self-centeredness, inability to see from others point-of-view, etc.

8. Resist the devil! Resist the temptation, no matter how things seem, to allow yourself to control or be controlled. Sometimes it seems easier to allow the abuse to continue, but God is not pleased if you allow the proliferation of a demonic stronghold in your life.

28

Warring Against Jezebel

Francis Frangipane tells of warring against the spirit of Jezebel
through prayer with his church. Right away several gays and
lesbians were delivered. Pastors and wives began calling to
confess sexual sins, and **persecution began**, mostly from people
who had been friends. One night the spirit of Jezebel manifested
at the foot of his bed and threatened to kill him and his church
members if he didn't stop praying against the Jezebel spirit.

One week later, a man called and threatened using the exact
words the demon had spoken. Jezebel had found a willing vessel.
Francis prayed for a snow storm that Saturday night and ten inches
fell by morning, so that very few people came to church. The ones
who did, prayed fervently and no one was harmed. Later, the man
who had threatened them got saved. (54)

The spirit of murder

Because Jezebel seeks to destroy the prophets and ministers of
God, one must be prayed up and never make a move without
God's armor firmly in place. I went to a woman's house at her
request to minister deliverance to her. For seven hours I prayed,
taught, encouraged, cast out demons, led her to the LORD and saw
glorious deliverance in her and her home. The next day her relatives began harassing and threatening me. Her mother was
"Queen Jezebel" over that family and **very** angry that I had
cleansed the house of demonic strongholds and gotten her
daughter delivered.

It turned out that the mother *owned* the house that her
daughter and grandchildren lived in and she *wanted* her daughter
in bondage. The daughter had been subjected to abuse from early
childhood and the mother wasn't going to let her escape so easily.

The daughter had begged me to carry off to a dumpster a number of objects from the home such as a statue she worshipped, a dream-catcher that was hung above her bed and gave her continual nightmares, voodoo jewelry, talismans, signs, and other objects. These demon infested objects were only part of the problem, but they were also a point of contact through which the family held the daughter in bondage. Because of her unstable, vulnerable state, they threatened to have her committed if she would not obey their wishes. In fear, she submitted once again to their control.

Though my family came under attack, we prayed and continued to plead the Blood of Jesus over ourselves, bind protective scriptures to ourselves and wear our armor. I noticed that stress and strife tried to enter our home, and fear practically stood on its head, trying to gain a foothold. We continued to stand until we saw the victory. We are to be strong in the LORD, not in our own understanding.

> **Finally, my brethren, be STRONG in the LORD, and in the power of HIS might. Put on the whole armor of God, that ye may be able to STAND against the WILES of the devil.** (*Ephesians 6:10-11*)

WILES is the word "methodia" in Greek. It means the following or pursuing of technical procedures in the handling of a subject. *You are the subject!* **STAND** is a military term. The devil wants you to "stand *down*." But YHWH *commands* you to "stand."

> **Wherefore take unto you the whole armor of God, that ye may be able to WITHSTAND in the evil day, and having done all, to STAND. STAND therefore...** (*Ephesians 6:13-14*)

Why do you suppose God commands us three times in this scripture to "stand?" Because He wants us to lie down and give up, or run in fear? Many times we wrestle with *ourselves* as much as we do the devil.

We allow our minds to entertain ungodly thoughts that end up in sin and thereby put holes in our armor. We remove our armor with sin. Unbelief is sin, too. To defeat Jezebel (or any other demon) we must take every thought captive, for the true battleground is in our own minds.

(For the weapons of our warfare are not carnal, but mighty through God to the pulling down of strongholds;) Casting down IMAGINATIONS, and every high thing that exalteth itself against the knowledge of God, and bringing into captivity every THOUGHT to the obedience of Christ... (*2 Corinthians 10:4-5*)

Notice, again, the allusion to warfare, but this time it is *our own thoughts* that need taming.

I was called to go to a woman's house who was suicidal, and a victim of satanic abuse. Interestingly enough, she had sliced up her wrists in a classic configuration, both vertical and horizontal (like the Baal prophets who ritually cut themselves). Problems erupted when I began to break the soul ties she had with coven members, her grandfather among them, who were her abusers. Once again, I discovered her parents, who had signed her over to the coven as a child, *owned* the house where we were. Deliverance needs to be done either in a "clean" place, such as a godly church, or with full permission and approval of the owners of the house. I cast out the demons, and the "power" that controlled her left when I prayed, but returned when I left. It had a right to be there, having been invited in by her parents.

Jezebel's worst nightmare

A humble, repentant people is a key to defeating Jezebel. She hates holiness (kodesh), the set-apart lifestyle of a godly man or woman. She despises the humility of a true servant and will seek to ridicule, humiliate and destroy the humble servant of the Most High. I know of an incident in which a leader bowed in repentance, with tears of humility, and was publicly rebuked by a person with a Jezebel spirit.

A true servant of God will manifest humility, not pride. A true servant doesn't mind humbling himself in public. Jezebel hates humility, holiness and those who expose her wickedness through example. Being conformed into Christ's likeness is an effectual weapon against this wicked spirit, coupled with speaking the Word with authority.

I beseech you therefore, brethren, by the mercies of God, that ye present your bodies a living sacrifice, holy,

acceptable unto God, which is your reasonable service. And **BE NOT CONFORMED TO THIS WORLD BUT BE YE TRANSFORMED BY THE RE-NEWING OF YOUR MIND...** (*Romans 12:1-2*)

BECAUSE WE HAVE FAILED TO SEE JEZEBEL IN OURSELVES AND OTHERS, WE HAVE NOT ALLOWED THE HOLY SPIRIT OF GOD TO CONVICT US OF THE SIN OF TOLERATING HER PRESENCE. We must be willing to trample her under the hooves of Jehu's horse! We must be willing to lament and repent in order to see our *own* failures and let the Holy Spirit bring change.

29

Holy Spirit Has Something Against Leaders Who Tolerate Jezebel

Each generation must answer for itself. The USA had revival at the turn of the 20th century. This is but a small spark compared to the glorious fire God is getting ready to turn loose at the beginning of the 21st century, the end of this age. God's fire will either cleanse us or destroy us, for it is an "All Consuming Fire." We are in a battle in which the leaders and pastors who stand against Jezebel may not be liked. They may be slandered, rejected and abused, yet they must stand up and expose the spiritual battle raging around us and declare the truth. If we don't turn things around *immediately,* our whole nation is set for judgment.

> **I have a few things against thee, because thou suf-ferest that woman Jezebel, which calleth herself a prophetess, to teach and to seduce my servants to commit fornication...And I GAVE HER SPACE TO REPENT of her fornication; and she repented not. Behold, I will cast her into a bed, and THEM THAT COMMIT ADULTERY WITH HER INTO GREAT TRIBULATION, except they repent of their deeds. And I WILL KILL HER CHILDREN WITH DEATH...** *(Revelation 2:20-23)*

God has given those with Jezebel spirits space to repent. She does not repent! God has given those who tolerate Jezebel space to repent. They will be cast into great tribulation with her. All who follow her and allow her seductions will be destroyed with her.

Leaders and pastors must stand up and say, "Jezebel is no longer welcome in our church! We stand against her wicked influence because we fear the LORD more than we fear her. It is YHWH we desire to please. We want to be a purified bride without spot or wrinkle. We are willing to lose finances if necessary, rather than entertain and coddle Jezebel. We will throw her and her minions out at any cost. No more false visions and dreams. No more wickedness. No more tolerance of evil. No more will we turn a blind eye, calling evil good and good evil. We repent of the sin of tolerating Jezebel in ourselves and others. We realize there are many false prophets—-and we fervently pray for discernment."

Steps to repentance for tolerating Jezebel

1. Ask for forgiveness for the sin of tolerating Jezebel in ourselves and in our midst.
2. Fight using the fruit of the spirit; peace, joy, self-control (temperance), faith, humility (meekness), goodness.
3. Where Jezebel brings confusion, bind to yourself a spirit of power and love and a sound mind.
4. Where she has brought fear, repent of fear and bind the fruit of the Spirit, faith, to yourself.
5. Where she has brought heaviness, lethargy and weakness, break this off and cast it out. Bind joy and the garment of praise to yourself.
6. This is not a war of the flesh, but of the Spirit. It requires humility, the cloak of zeal for righteousness, and destruction spoken to all the workings of this enemy of God. This is accomplished through sincere repentance, prayer and fasting. The servant of God must be pure, without blame, so the devil has no room for accusation.
7. Jezebel brings the debacle of our moral standards.
     a. Rebuke these manifestations.
     b. Repent of allowing immorality and idolatry to replace true worship.
8. In every area of life where the Jezebel influence has brought weakness, ask for mercy, and bind strengthening scriptures to yourself.

God's promise to those who overcome Jezebel is to grant power over the nations. Look at *Revelation 2:26*:

And he that overcometh, and keepeth My works UNTO THE END, to him will I give POWER OVER THE NATIONS...

30

Steps For Deliverance From A Jezebel Spirit

Though I have referred to the Jezebel spirit as a she, it can use *anyone*. If you have been under bondage to a Jezebel spirit, pray using the steps outlined below.

1. Pray fervently.
2. Seek help from a minister who does not operate with a controlling spirit.
3. Bind up the Jezebel spirit, and all its seductions and operations through you.
4. Plead the blood of Yahshua (Jesus) over yourself.
5. Put on the whole armor of YHWH (God). *(Ephesians 6:11-17)*
6. Renounce all association with Jezebel in Yahshua's (Jesus') Name.
7. Cast out this demon and break its influence off your life. You will almost certainly need help with this.
8. Repent of the love for ungodly power and for allowing this demon to operate through you.
9. If you have a Jezebel spirit, there is always mercy in allowing yourself to be conformed to the image of Christ.
10. Submit to authority, and allow them to help you and show you a better way.
11. This battle must be fought in the spirit, not through the flesh: The flesh *must* lose.
12. You must break free to fulfill God's plan for your life, by doing the opposite of what this spirit dictates. Remember that strongholds in your mind are holding you hostage to ungodly thought patterns.

13. The ultimate answer is humility, and must be sought carefully with tears. *Humility is our defense!* Much repentance is needed.
14. Bind humility to yourself. Listen to the two songs on the *"Heart & Soul Surrender"* album, *"I Surrender Myself"* and *"Heart & Soul."* These songs bring an anointing for repentance, total surrender of the heart (a key to deliverance from a Jezebel spirit), and the spirit of humility. Also, listen to the dramatic work, *"Nails,"* on the same album, for deliverance.
15. Cast out a controlling spirit, a spirit of seduction, a spirit of whoredoms, an anti-Christ spirit, deception, manipulation, a lying spirit, witchcraft, divination, lethargy, a spirit of murder, slumber, error, haughtiness and familiar spirits.
16. Renounce and sever all connections, soul ties and cabal-tows to the demonic realm.
17. Smash every stronghold and trigger that might draw you back into manipulation and power-play (witchcraft), characteristic of Jezebel.
18. Ask God's forgiveness, and plead the blood over yourself.
19. Pray for strength and wisdom. Ask the LORD to soften your heart.
20. Let the Holy Spirit search your heart in a time of fasting and prayer. Ask Him to show you areas where you have been a manipulator. Then repent.
21. Bind appropriate scriptures to yourself concerning humility, peace, and love. Fill yourself up with the Word, especially 1 Corinthians 13, *Amplified Bible.*

31

Bitter-Root Judgments Open Door to Jezebel

Bitter-root judgments can compel a person to fulfill in his/her own life the very thing he/she judged in others. Bitter-root judgments are made against offenders and compel a person, through the law of sowing and reaping, to reap the same judgments back in his/her own life. The catch is that the reaping is greater than the sowing.

A woman who judges men (perhaps her father) for being abusive, harsh and unloving, will become the same way through reaping what she has sown. She welcomes Jezebel as an avenging angel for the injustices she feels she has suffered. She becomes a controller because of fear. She must give up manipulative behavior, learn to trust God and take every thought captive to the obedience of Christ. *(2 Corinthians 10:4-5)*

(For an in–depth explanation on this subject matter get my book or tape entitled *Bitter-Root Judgments, Inner Vows and Soul Ties*.)

Steps for deliverance from bitter-root judgments

1. Seek help from a minister who does not operate with a controlling spirit.
2. Repent wholeheartedly for allowing Jezebel to operate through you.
3. Renounce all involvement with Jezebel.
4. Cast out the Jezebel spirit, and all other spirits operating with her. (See previous chapter)
5. Submit to a time of correction; learn to trust again.
6. Ask God's forgiveness, and plead the blood over yourself.

7. Pray for strength and wisdom. Ask the LORD to soften your heart.
8. Break every bitter-root judgment you have made, especially against parents, relatives and spouses.
9. Bind humility to yourself and learn to operate in the fruit of the spirit.
10. Let the Holy Spirit search your heart in a time of fasting and prayer. Ask Him to show you areas where you have been a manipulator.
11. Repent and renounce witchcraft and manipulation.
12. Follow all other steps for deliverance in the previous chapter.

32

Some Characteristics of Jezebel

Spotting Jezebel

I overheard a budding prophetess state, "I can spot 'Jezi's' a mile away!" What arrogance! It takes time to "know them by their fruit." Meanwhile, Jezebel is fleecing the flock, destroying the faith and trust of many while leading God's people into sin and idolatry. I know of a church where it was several years before the pastor's past came up to haunt him. No one knew about the fraud and embezzlement that was prevalent in other congregations he had pastored, until an incident arose that led to an investigation.

On the other hand, I know of a man who was trained and sent in by a witch coven from a western state. He ripped up a small but godly church in a matter of five weeks, taking half of the congregation with him. When the pastors began to check, they discovered he had attempted to destroy another church in Oklahoma before coming to Missouri and targeting them. This Jezebel's new "church" fell apart quickly, leaving several sheep permanently devastated. Then he moved on to a new place to start the process all over again.

Recently, I ministered to a congregation in a small town where Jezebel had ruled the roost for several years before the new pastor arrived. She and her husband controlled the board of elders and the finance committee. She controlled her husband by withholding intimacy and refusing to clean or cook. He was forced to hire a maid who cleaned around her as she sat in her recliner. On Sunday mornings she would stand up and order the elders to sit down, which they did like whipped puppies. The new pastor was able to have her voted out, but half of the people and most of the finances went with her. For revenge, she called family services and through false accusations, took away the pastor's son. The night I was there we broke Jezebel's stronghold and curses she had made against the people. Many repented of bitterness and unforgiveness, and great numbers were healed emotionally and physically. To God be the glory!

Ye shall know them by their fruits... *(Matthew 7:16)*

A good tree cannot bring forth evil fruit, neither can a corrupt tree bring forth good fruit. Every tree that bringeth not forth good fruit is hewn down, and cast into the fire. Wherefore by their fruits ye shall know them. *(Matthew 7:18-20)*

Following is a list of characteristics that often accompany Jezebels, but to keep from being deceived, the best guard is unequivocally a deep relationship with the LORD. There is a *knowing* that comes with experience, and discernment from the Holy Spirit.

Characteristics: May vary

1. Jezebel is a liar
2. Jezebel is a deceiver (anything goes to achieve her goals)
   a. Uses deceit to destroy many
   b. Jezebel herself is deeply deceived
3. Jezebel thinks nothing of bearing false witness to get her way
4. Jezebel is ruthless
5. Jezebel is heartless
6. Jezebel is a backstabber
7. Jezebel is a usurper
8. Jezebel is wicked (which means twisted)
9. Jezebel will not answer righteous questions that would expose her and the truth
   a. She answers with evasion, deftly twisting the truth and facts
   b. She does not repent, even with the truth right in her face
   c. She always has an excuse for her behavior, no matter how outrageous
10. Jezebel targets worship leaders, pastors, elders, dancers, people in authority and their spouses, etc.
11. Jezebel prefers refined qualities but will use anyone
12. Jezebel hates humility
13. Jezebel hates repentance
14. Jezebel hates true holiness
15. Jezebel causes some pastors to be controlling and unyielding
16. Jezebel is not accountable to others (pastor, spouse, etc.)
17. Jezebel, if in a man, is flirtatious with women
18. Jezebel may be adulterous

19. Jezebel prefers the traits of women, primarily
20. Jezebel has excessive prophetic "words," prophecies, dreams and visions
21. Jezebel manifests constant *false* "words" and prophecies
22. Jezebel is obsessed with prophecies & dreams/ talks about them constantly, instead of more sure Word of prophecy, the Bible
23. Jezebel causes others to have false dreams and prophecies by laying on of hands and imparting unclean spirits
24. Jezebel is intensely ambitious
25. Jezebel maneuvers into leadership positions in order to control
26. Jezebel is a control freak
27. Jezebel uses others to achieve her own ends
28. Jezebel is a despot, a tyrant
29. Jezebel is a murderer
30. Jezebel is a whore
31. Jezebel promotes false religion
32. Jezebel lets nothing stand in the way of what she desires
33. Jezebel changes or bends the law or rules to suit her own ends
34. Jezebel believes she is *above* the law and the rules
35. Jezebel believes the end justifies the means
36. Jezebel pretends to be doing what is right
37. Jezebel only *pretends* to be doing the king's will
38. Jezebel is fiercely independent
39. Jezebel pretends to desire to protect and help others
40. Jezebel turns followers into eunuchs and zombies
41. Jezebel drains the life out of her victims
42. Others feel helpless to fight against her
43. She divides in order to conquer
    a. She keeps people at one another's throats through her lies and deceptions
    b. She attempts to keep the parties apart so strife will continue and she can manipulate the result
    c. She destroys evidence that proves innocence of her victims
44. Jezebel nit-picks to find fault and drive her enemies crazy, sometimes badgering them to distraction
45. Jezebel questions the integrity of others in order to discredit them
46. Jezebel sees herself as lofty, much higher than the sheep
47. Jezebel calls herself a prophetess or prophet
48. Jezebel is proud
49. She claims superior holiness
50. Jezebel is a master of camouflage
51. Jezebel is a wolf in sheep's clothing
52. Jezebel is a predator

53. Jezebel is a man-hater
54. Jezebel has contempt for the weak
55. There will be inconsistencies in Jezebel's stories
56. Jezebel seeks recognition
57. Jezebel is greedy

Personality traits of Jezebel: May vary individually

1. Excessive chatter or moody and brooding
2. Time waster, procrastinator of godly projects
3. No humility
4. Highlights self
5. Forcefully steers conversations
6. Brags of the hours spent interceding
7. Exhibitionist
8. Fears exposure
9. Silences true prophets
10. Attacks true prophets with devastating false words
11. Tries to humiliate true prophets, publicly and privately
12. Excessive jealousy or competitiveness
13. The Jezebel's who fool you the longest are the most ruthless and dangerous
14. Jezebel appears pious
15. Look at her lifestyle
    a. Personal life screwed up; may be carefully hidden—takes time
16. Builds up to *offering* the whole night
17. Twists scripture to justify actions, such as:
    a. *If you receive a prophet in the name of a prophet, you will receive a prophet's reward.*
    b. True prophets don't need to extort money, constantly reminding people of the widow and son who gave their last meal to Elijah.
18. *Seems* genuine, but is spiritually *off*
19. Jezebel has mixture in her spirit
20. Jezebel controls the money
21. Jezebel's money is a snare for the weak and for Ahabs / it is also a way to *control* pastors, churches, families...
22. Establishes authority by controlling others
    a. Won't allow others to speak in conversation
    b. Constantly interrupts in order to distract and dominate conversations
    c. Dominates conversations
23. Sometimes she uses a loud voice to interrupt or brag——really subtle ones know this is a dead giveaway and avoid loud talk

24. Uses *another's* name to gain control or promote her own agenda
25. Plots and carries out destruction of the righteous and innocent
26. Relentless and savage in her relationships and business dealings
27. Sarcastic and derogatory
28. Backstabs and bears tales
29. Quick to anger
30. Anxious, hyper
31. No peace / no joy / frustrated / upset (tries to hide it)
32. Always full of plans, plans, plans/ always on the go/ *looks* like she's busy for the LORD
33. Coercing everyone
34. Fast talking and nervous (covers up true motivation)
35. Jezebel will attack immediately when threatened
    a. She foments lies and counter-accusations
    b. She hits hard and heavy
36. Jezebel *has been* operating with complete anonymity
37. Uses seduction to manipulate
38. There is no peace around Jezebel
39. Jezebel brings a spirit of confusion, division and strife
40. Pretends to be a worshipper and intercessor
41. Aligns herself with true prophets to give credence to her agenda

Jezebel's agenda:

1. False prophecy
2. Slaughter of innocent
3. Kill or discredit true prophets
4. Abortion
5. Destroy family
6. Homosexuality
7. Pornography
8. Brings spirit of slumber
9. Lull people into:
    a. Complacency
    b. Apathy
    c. Submission to wickedness
10. Take control through another
11. Promote false religion or error
12. Introduce the occult
13. Spirit of murder, rage, hatred
14. Antichrist spirit turns hearts away from true worship
15. Attempts to create focus on herself
16. May lie down and sleep when frustrated (even snore) in attempt to gain attention or usurp authority

Jezebel hates:

1. Prayer
2. Humility, self–control
3. Repentance
4. Faith, peace
5. True prophets and prophecy
6. Truth
7. Manifested fruit of the spirit

Jezebel causes:

1. Fear, timidity, stress, strife
2. Physical weakness
3. Discouragement
4. Guilt
5. Feelings of helplessness
6. Bondage to porn
7. Insatiable sexual desire
8. Holy Spirit to be quenched
9. False accusations
10. Threats
11. Murder
12. Abortion
13. Frustration
14. Moral failure
15. Idolatry

Jezebel manipulates through:

1. Anger or silence
2. Money or financial control
3. Domination—won't live with anyone she can't dominate
4. Yields in her heart to no one
5. Owns and/or manipulates media
6. Counter-attacks
7. Fierce independence
8. Strife and division
9. Seduction
10. Confusion
11. Deceit
12. Slander
13. Lies
14. Vengefulness
15. Carefully orchestrated plan of attack

Part Four

The Ahab Spirit

And it came to pass, as if it had been a light thing for him to walk in the sins of Jeroboam...that he took to wife Jezebel...and went and served Baal, and worshipped him. *1 Kings 16:31*

33

The Sins of Ahab

Ahab's sins come down on whole nation

Ahab was the son of Omri (meaning servant of YHWH), and he was the seventh king of Israel. Omri did more evil than all that were before him. Ahab means "father's brother," and in his twenty-two year reign he surely:

> ...did more evil in the sight of the LORD above all that were before him. (*1 Kings 16:30*)

When leaders are wrong and wicked, the whole country suffers pollution and demon infestation through them. This also applies to churches, businesses and homes. America should be very careful whom they elect to public office.

Ahab's sins are a light thing to him

Ahab sinned as if it was a light thing when he married the heathen Jezebel, but he could have taken his proper authority in the home and over the country. His greatest sin was forsaking the one true God and allowing Jezebel to practice and spread Baal worship. Elijah said to Ahab:

> I have not troubled Israel; but thou, and thy father's house, in that ye have forsaken the commandments of the LORD, and thou hast followed Baalim. (*1 Kings 18:18*)

Despite the fact that Jezebel introduced Baal worship, it is Ahab who is held responsible. He is the one who:

> ...reared up an altar for Baal in the house of Baal, which he had built in Samaria. And Ahab

made a grove (pagan shrine for pleasure); and Ahab did more to provoke the LORD God of Israel to anger than all the kings of Israel that were before him. (*1 Kings 16:32-33*)

God was merciful to Ahab over and over, sending the Word of the LORD through Elijah, and for a time he even repented. But his repentance was little more than that of Jezebel's eunuch.

Ahab lusts for material possessions

Ahab probably should have killed Benhadad, instead of making a lucrative deal with him. He lusted for Naboth's vineyard, whining to Jezebel. She had Naboth killed to satisfy Ahab's competitive lust, while he behaved like a baby, relentlessly seeking for bigger and better things. The child on his way to being an Ahab will be attacked by Satan with rejection and wounds, and he will be fearful of relationships. He may lose or be rejected by his father.

Ahab is a dichotomy

Ahab often comes off schizophrenic. Because he is under Jezebel's power, he is alternately explosive then apologetic, or whiny then angry, etc. He is deeply confused because he is torn in different directions. He eagerly wants to please, but he can't decide just who to please first. He *rarely* makes the right choice: To please YHWH first. He is frustrated, longing for someone to simply *put him out of his misery and tell him what to do.* Jezebel is only too happy to oblige.

Where there's a Jezebel there's an Ahab

Where there is a Jezebel one *will* find an Ahab. In the case where the pastor of a church has a Jezebel spirit, the *whole church* is defiled by serving as the Ahab. Ahab enables Jezebel to function. Jezebel floods her victim with weakness and help-lessness, walking on them until they can't hold up their heads without shame. They become ineffectual eunuchs after submitting to Jezebel's tyranny. Ahab's will be fearful and resentful, dominated by Jezebel.

Symbiotic relationship

Jezebel and Ahab are intertwined spiritually. They are co-dependant. A man with an Ahab spirit who divorces his wife will unwittingly marry into the same problems again. Jezebel will seek a spouse whom she can dominate through sheer force of character.

Having conquered Ahab, Jezebel was not going to stop at merely becoming queen. She wanted to rule, and she married the correct weakling to accomplish her goal. These are really Satan's goals: to destroy families, kingdoms and churches through subtly changing the direction of worship of the one true God and substitute, through deception, idolatry. In a Jezebel controlled congregation, the song service will be happy, happy, relentlessly upbeat, never venturing toward songs about deep repentance, or the cleansing blood of Yahshua. Ahab was a willing participant in Jezebel's schemes because of his many shortcomings as a leader.

Elder boards, deacon boards and boards of directors in churches or ministries should watch carefully. These are perfect places for a Jezebel/Ahab combination to hide out and do their work without being brought into the light. Once a Jezebel/Ahab has control of the purse strings, it is very easy for them to sit in the dark, cutting God's plans out of the churches' vision and budget.

Who is making all the decisions on placement of funds, when programs with God's anointing clearly on them get cut out of the budget? Allocating funds for building projects is frequently used as a strategy to take money out of the hands of God's youth ministries, orphan and widow programs, evangelistic thrusts, and any other ministry that would forcefully advance the kingdom of YHWH into Satan's territory.

Instead, plans for the largest, most decadent edifice (church building) in town eats up the provision, time and efforts of a whole community of believers for several years. By the time the building project is over, God's Spirit has moved on, and Jezebel has a fine new building to be proud of.

Vanity becomes Jezebel, but heaven help the believers that are deceived, seduced and enticed to enter into Jezebel's abominations. Heading toward godliness, righteousness and true holiness are simply not on Jezebel's agenda.

Infiltration by covens

A common occurrence among covens and satanic groups is to train people to infiltrate churches and engineer their downfall from within. A few years ago I discovered that a particularly energetic group in Arizona had dispatched people throughout the USA. They succeeded in destroying several churches. I had the displeasure of meeting one of these people. He appeared at a church and immediately began to worm his way into the pastor's confidence. When the time was right, this man suddenly stood up to the pastor, denouncing him and exposing his weaknesses. He took several sheep with him and started another fellowship.

About a year later another man began attending the same church. He played up to the pastors, becoming their chief sycophant, while befriending other strategic people in the church. It took several months to work out his plan, but eventually, he openly attacked the pastors (along with others who had become his supporters) and their doctrine, broke their hearts, and destroyed the church. (It should be noted that both of these infiltrators had done the same thing in other cities.)

Sometimes pastors and leaders are vulnerable because of sheep-bite and other wounds they have suffered. They feel lonely, isolated and in need of friendship. Carefully coached Jezebels take advantage of such leaders to acquire information they can use to their advantage. They learn the weaknesses and strengths of their targets, while plotting an attack. Sometimes, the infiltrators leave to start another church and manage to take a number of the sheep with them.

I know of at least fifteen incidents in various churches where this scenario took place. In more than one of these churches Jezebel was allowed to dance lewdly in front of the church at every service, but she was the pastor's friend and confidant so it was allowed.

Sometimes, if a leader is known to have a weakness in the sexual arena, he/she will be targeted by SEDUCTIVE persons who are trained and sent in by covens or inspired by the devil himself. Leaders should beware, never allowing themselves to be compromised in this way. Men, don't counsel women alone and guard your heart carefully. Work at keeping your marriage healthy, spending quality time with your spouse.

Now the Spirit speaketh expressly, that in the latter times some shall depart from the faith, giving heed to

SEDUCING SPIRITS, and doctrines of devils; Speaking lies in hypocrisy; having their conscience seared with a hot iron... (*1 Timothy 4:1-2*)

Don't allow the hurts, rejections and wounds of life to fester. Take them to the Father. Repent. Otherwise, right in the middle of your pity party, you may find yourself embroiled in sexual scandal. It has happened to many otherwise godly men and women, and without the supernatural strength and protection of the LORD, it could happen to you! Numerous leaders, both small and great, have fallen prey to Jezebel's seductions.

34
Home Out of Order

No stomach for the tough decisions

An Ahab controlled husband may take his resentment out on other females in the work place, behaving in a critical and abusive manner. His home is out of order, and he feels helpless to stop it. In his heart there is a spirit of murder, but he feels impotent, unable to bring change. Ahab was unable to stand up to Jezebel after the contest on Mount Carmel, missing a golden opportunity to right the wrongs in his household and his kingdom.

In a mighty show of His power, YHWH delivered the Syrians into Ahab's hand, but Ahab spared the life of Ben-hadad, the Syrian king who blasphemed YHWH by calling Him a mere god of the hills, but not of the valleys. Ahab made a covenant with Ben-hadad instead of destroying him. Ahab committed treasonous acts under Jezebel's influence as any man will under her spell.

When a certain son of the prophets confronted Ahab and pronounced a death sentence on him for this treasonous act, he went home heavy, downhearted and displeased. Just as everything seemed to be going well for Ahab, and he had a chance to do something right, it always turned sour because of his weakness of character. No wonder God sent the fearsome Elijah and Jehu to clean up Ahab's messes.

Nowhere to hide

God sees all that we do. He will not be mocked. The illegal extortion of Naboth's vineyard is a case in point. Because Ahab sowed to the wind, and acted out his sinful, carnal desires by seizing that which is precious to God, a man's inheritance, he reaped to the whirlwind, through the destruction of *his* inheritance, his sons and his throne.

David also angered God with his willful lusts of the flesh. The whole incident with Bathsheba caused the death of their first child together, and many lives were lost in Israel as a result of his sin.

David took Bathsheba, who was precious to Uriah, to use for his own lusts. It is only David's sincere repentance that saved him and his house.

Notice that when Ahab repented, it was to save his own hide, mostly for show, but God looks on the heart. He gave Ahab, who didn't possess the strength of character to repent sincerely, or walk in a godly way before a kodesh (holy, set apart) God, only a temporary reprieve.

> **...because he humbleth himself before Me, I will not bring the evil in his days: but in his son's days will I bring the evil upon his house.** (*1 Kings 21:29*)

If David had received this word, he would have sought the LORD carefully, with many tears. God sees our true heart-condition, not the phony one we present to the world.

Ahab considers things of God trivial

Ahab abdicated his place of authority to Jezebel, refusing to follow the true God or His prophets. With all his wealth, he had wrong desires which opened him up to sin and exposed him to vexation, all because he considered the things of God trivial.

Ahab vulnerable to perversion

Ahab married Jezebel both because it was politically strategic and because he was attracted to her forceful personality. She enhanced her beauty by painting her eyes, which the holy (kodesh) women of her day did not do. As a high priestess of Baal, she was probably into perverse sex, which would be alluring to a weak king such as Ahab. Through her manipulations and charms, she maneuvered herself into the power position, usurping Ahab's authority. She was the Baal prostitute who led all Israel into sin.

Ahab abdicates

Ahab will not fulfill the role of leadership in his home, refusing to set a good example for the children, dumping responsibilities on the wife that he should handle. An Ahab becomes a passive quitter, ever weaker as he goes. The wife tries to take up the slack becoming progressively stronger. The more he abdicates, the more she will take up the slack, until she is in complete control. Even though Ahab has abdicated authority, *he* will be the one held accountable by God. Disorder in the home brings the curse of God. This can result in broken homes, children sometimes becoming homosexuals, or following the perversions of the parents. (33)

I know of many men who wind up in adulterous relationships because they feel like frustrated failures at home. This manifests in financial, spiritual, emotional and relational problems. They justify the adultery because they don't feel appreciated or understood at home. Often, it becomes a way to vent frustration and deep-seated anger over the guilt and shame of their inability to provide godly leadership.

Repentance from an Ahab spirit

1. Repent of sympathy for Jezebel.
2. Repent of yielding to an Ahab spirit, and allowing it to operate through you. If Ahab is a whole church, the congregation must repent.
3. Ask God's forgiveness for failure to take your proper place in God's plan.
4. Bind up the Ahab spirit's power to operate over yourself and your home. Break this evil influence over your mind.
5. Repent of bitter-root judgments and inner vows made in your youth against aggressive, Jezebelian mothers and fathers.
6. Separate yourself from Jezebel's influence.
7. Hate the garment even spotted by the fleshly sin of following Jezebel.
8. Repent for succumbing to spiritual and perhaps physical adultery.

Deliverance from an Ahab spirit

1. Put on the whole armor of God, that you may be able to withstand the fiery darts of the wicked one.
2. Renounce this evil spirit.
3. Cast out the Ahab and Jezebel spirit.
4. Be strong in the LORD and the power of "His" might. Stand and resist!
5. Break every stronghold off your family, home and church. There will be complex structures (strongholds to break) and this will require time, persistence and faithfulness.

6. Cast out a spirit of fear. Resist the devil, and the temptation to yield or waver under the attacks of Jezebel.

7. Bind a spirit of power and love and a sound mind to yourself.

8. Get proper authority in place and don't *yield* to the easy way out.

9. Fast and pray for wisdom on how to handle Jezebel.

10. Take back the headship of your home in a firm but loving manner.

11. Remember: *Loving leadership is not about domination.* (57)

12. Realize that you didn't get in this situation overnight, and you won't get out of it overnight. Be patient.

13. Stand fast, strengthening and encouraging yourself in the Word.

14. Eat protein for strength. If you are attacked with weakness, bind scriptures to yourself for strength such as:

But they that wait upon the LORD shall renew their strength; they shall mount up with wings as eagles; they shall run, and not be weary; and they shall walk, and not faint. (*Isaiah 40:31*)

15. Remember, if you sincerely desire to break the power of Jezebel and Ahab off your life, God will send His angels to protect you. Bind Luke 10:19 to yourself at all times.

Behold, I give unto you power to tread on serpents and scorpions, and over all the power of the enemy: and nothing shall by any means hurt you. (*Luke 10:19*)

16. Plead the blood over yourself, your household and church, daily. Play Christian music in your home.

17. *Expect* YHWH to move in your behalf. Rejoice!

If any of you lack wisdom, let him ask of God, that giveth to all men liberally, and upbraideth not; and it shall be given him. (*James 1:5*)

18. Put on your armor and don't take it off!

19. Use your faith to stand!

Wherefore take unto you the whole armor of God, that ye may be able to WITHSTAND in the evil day, and having done all, to STAND. STAND therefore... (*Ephesians 6:13-14*)

Part Five

The Spirit of Elijah

Behold, I will send you Elijah the prophet before the coming of the great and dreadful day of the LORD: And he shall turn the heart of the fathers to the children, and the heart of the children to their fathers, lest I come and smite the earth with a curse. *Malachi 4:5-6*

35

Fire and Rain

Elijah (meaning El YHWH, or Almighty God) was Jezebel's nemesis and strongest opponent. Because of the wickedness in the land, YHWH raised up one of His most powerful prophets, Elijah. He appeared suddenly, out of nowhere, a solitary voice against the evil King Ahab and Queen Jezebel, and was the grandest character Israel ever produced.

When he shut the heavens, God protected him continually, hiding and feeding him on numerous occasions, showing him the faithful, loving care of a kodesh (holy, set-apart) God. When, in her rage against the drought prophesied by Elijah, Jezebel ordered the murder of the prophets of YHWH, Elijah was cared for by the LORD's hand, fed by a raven at the brook Cherith, and later by a widow in Zarephath. God, then as now, protects His own true servants.

Time in the wilderness

God must train every one that He loves. This is not optional. Our time alone with Him in wilderness experiences is more precious than a thousand Mount Carmels, for it is here that we learn to follow our Shepherd's voice. It is here that we are molded into obedient and trusted servants, without which we are little more than presumptuous fools. He must train each individual to trust Him for needs to be met, and to move in the courts of kings, not as a mere man, but as a representative of the Most High. He must get the city (lusts of the flesh, pride of life, cares of this life) out of the man, so therefore He takes the man out of the city into the wilderness experiences.

As many as I love, I rebuke and chasten: be zealous therefore, and repent. (*Revelation 3:19*)

Paul, the Apostle, spent several years in the Arabian desert. John the Baptist spent much time in the desert living on locusts and honey. Moses was in the desert for forty years, and then spent forty more with the Hebrews wandering in the desert. God told Abraham to leave Ur, and then kept him wandering in the wilderness the rest of his life.

> **Whose fan is in His hand, and He will thoroughly purge His floor, and will gather the wheat into His garner; but the chaff he will burn with fire unquenchable.** (*Luke 3:17*)

"One with God is a majority" (Martin Luther)

Elijah was a rugged individual who stood alone and didn't voice public opinion. His fiery zeal was not popular in his day nor well received by kings or the people. They viewed him as one would an exotic but dangerous animal.

Through the brilliant triumph on Mount Carmel, he exposed the infection of Baal worship in the land of Israel for what it was, a festering sore that would bring death and destruction to God's chosen people. He compelled the people to stare the truth in the face. YHWH knew it would take this kind of in-your-face prophet to shake the people out of their slumber and idolatry.

Fire and rain

When Elijah returns again he will be hated and reviled for bringing judgment, calling fire down from heaven, and stopping the rains once more. The Elijah spirit is a forerunner spirit and it is come again to this wicked land, to expose all darkness, to risk everything in an all or nothing contest between the forces of darkness and light. The people must once again choose: Face total destruction, the survivors carried away into death or slavery; or turn with white-hot fervent repentance, prayer and fasting before the living God before it's too late.

36
Elijah the Revolutionary

Elijah's prophecies brought drought and famine (no dew or rain for three and a half years). The time of Elijah's ministry was not a comfortable season for Israel. Ahab and the people blamed Elijah, but he pointed out that it was Ahab's sin that brought punishment, and the increasing worship of idols. All the king and people had to do was repent, but they blamed God's prophet instead.

> **And Elijah the Tishbite, who was of the inhabitants of Gilead, said unto Ahab, As the LORD God of Israel liveth, before whom I stand, there shall not be dew nor rain these years, but according to my word. (*1 Kings 17:1*)**

Elijah returned and challenged the king. Please notice that Elijah didn't directly address Jezebel. He spoke to Ahab because Ahab was responsible for allowing Jezebel to operate. God was pleading with Ahab to do right through the use of the drought.

> **And it came to pass, when Ahab saw Elijah, that Ahab said unto him, Art thou he that troubleth Israel? And he answered, I have not troubled Israel; but thou, and thy father's house, in that ye have forsaken the commandments of the LORD, and thou hast followed Baalim. (*1 Kings 18:17-18*)**

The confrontation

Mount Carmel was the perfect location for the dramatic confrontation between Baal, the pagan weather deity, and YHWH.

From high on top this mountain they could look out on the magnificent rolling valleys below and realize they were part of something greater than themselves. This was the place where Canaanites had built temples to Baal and Ashtoreth and one of the places Israelites came to worship Baal.

The confrontation settled many issues for it was also between Jezebel (and her prophets) and Elijah. When Jezebel lost she did not take it lying down. She fought back with fury, just as the spirit of Jezebel does today.

37

The End-Time Laodicean Church

> So then because thou art lukewarm, and neither cold nor hot, I will spew thee out of my mouth. *(Revelation 3:16)*

When Elijah confronted the prophets of Baal on Mount Carmel, it became a grand scale struggle of epic proportions. Elijah challenged:

> How long halt ye between two opinions? if the LORD be God, follow Him: but if Baal, then follow him. And the people answered him not a word. *(1 Kings 18:21)*

The wavering, double-mindedness of the people was exposed and confronted, but they gave no answer. Not only didn't they have an answer, they were not ashamed of their failure to know and to do what is right. They stared dumbly at Elijah, waiting for "THE SHOW" to begin, and what a show it was.

> Hear me, O LORD, hear me, that this people may know that Thou art the LORD God, and that Thou hast turned their heart back again. Then the fire of the LORD fell, and consumed the burnt sacrifice, and the wood, and the stones, and the dust, and licked up the water that was in the trenches. And when all the people saw it, they fell on their faces: and they said, The LORD, He is the God; the LORD, He is the God. *(1 Kings 18:37-39)*

All the people were riding fences. They refused to speak or commit to one side or the other. They were neither hot nor cold, for they had a wishy-washy king with no backbone. **They came because of curiosity, not conviction.**

The same conditions exist today. There have been many times when I've stood before a group of people and challenged them to stand in faith and believe. I know how Elijah must have felt, for I have been stared down by haughty, religious fence-riders, both young and old, for years. I have learned, the hard way, to ignore how people look and act and simply do what YHWH tells me to do. This refusal to back down from God's commands has brought me persecution, but believe me, this is better than refusing to follow YHWH. The Father has chastened me for giving up and laying down my sword, and I never want to go through that kind of discipline again. It is far preferable to be *alone* following YHWH's directions, than to come under the fearsome hand of His displeasure.

Sadly, many pastors are in love with their comfortable jobs, and don't want to rock the boat. The devil sends Jezebels into the midst of modern day congregations to deceive and destroy weak leaders and people, until there is no urgency, no fervency, no passion left.

The Laodicean end-time church

As God's people languish in apathy and become experts at riding the fence, the LORD again confronts them with a choice. His people still silently wait for a "show" or a sign from heaven, rather than believe and boldly proclaim the LORD is the one true God.

I know thy works, that thou art neither cold nor hot: I would thou wert cold or hot. So then because thou art LUKEWARM, and neither cold nor hot, I will spew thee out of my mouth. (*Revelation 3:15-16*)

In Elijah's time the people had to make a choice. This generation must also make a choice. Love pleasure more than God; or take up the cross daily and follow Christ, the Messiah.

A further proof of YHWH's powerful hand on Elijah was when he outran Ahab's chariot. From Carmel to Jezreel was 25 miles. Men and women of God in our time will do great exploits, as well. People want to run like Elijah, and those who overcome Jezebel will run and not be weary and walk and not faint. They shall mount up with wings as eagles.

From elation to fear and rejection

After great exploits, in a state of exhaustion, Jezebel's threats caused Elijah to run again, not in victory this time, but in fear, to the farthest, southernmost city of Judah: Beersheba. He went an additional day's journey as he fled to the wilderness. Panic, despondency and self-pity reared their ugly heads.

It seemed for a long moment as if Jezebel had won, but God had other plans. An angel brought Elijah food and water twice. On those two meals he went forty days and nights to the very mountain where YHWH had revealed Himself to Moses and the children of Israel.

Jezebel's threats *seem* to be a harbinger of defeat, but God can turn our worst personal failures into victories. God spoke to Elijah and comforted him. He gave him instructions and soon Elijah was back in his element, speaking God's Word, calling fire down from heaven and bringing destruction to the enemies of YHWH.

38

The Day of the LORD Is At Hand!

These are the days of Elijah

Yahshua Messiah proclaimed *(Matthew 17)* that Elijah will return before the great and terrible day of the LORD. Elijah and Jezebel were real people, but on a deeper level are symbols, types and shadows of intense and powerful events *yet to come*, foreshadowed in God's Word. The spirit of Jezebel and the spirit of Elijah dwell in America today. The whirlwind of judgment is at the door, for it has reached the fullness of time.

Elijah, the prophet of power, prepared the way for the people to receive YHWH. John the Baptist prepared the way for the Messiah. Both Elijah and the Messiah were RECEIVED into heaven (raptured) alive.

> **So then after the Lord had spoken unto them, He was RECEIVED UP into heaven, and sat on the right hand of God. (*Mark 16:19*)**

> **And it came to pass, as they still went on, and talked, that, behold, there appeared a chariot of fire, and horses of fire, and parted them both asunder; and Elijah WENT UP by a whirlwind into heaven. (*2 Kings 2:11*)**

The prophetic is "rising up" again in the people of God. The harvest is ripe for souls and wickedness abounds, ready for Elijah to arise again and jolt them out of their complacency.

> **Put ye in the sickle, for the HARVEST IS RIPE: come, get you down: for the press is full, the VATS OVERFLOW; for their WICKEDNESS IS GREAT. (*Joel 3:13*)**

The time for indolence and apathy is over for God's fullness has come. The harvest is ripe but the laborers are few.

Multitudes, multitudes in the valley of decision: for the day of the LORD is near in the valley of decision. (*Joel 3:14*)

We sing, "Send your fire," and our hearts long to see it, but we don't grasp the full implications of that fire.

And Elijah answered and said to the captain of fifty, If I be a man of God, then let fire come down from heaven, and consume thee and thy fifty. And there CAME DOWN FIRE FROM HEAVEN AND CONSUMED HIM and his fifty. (*2 Kings 1:10*)

The "All Consuming Fire" is not a play thing we can take lightly. It is the power of YHWH to destroy sin and bring revival. First, the sin must be repented of or the people will be destroyed when the anointing fire for true revival comes. This is the fire of cleansing, a necessary first step!

...Let the bridegroom go forth of his chamber and the bride out of her closet. Let the priests, and ministers of the LORD, WEEP BETWEEN THE PORCH AND ALTAR, and let them say, SPARE THY PEOPLE, O LORD, AND GIVE NOT THINE HERITAGE TO RE- PROACH, THAT THE HEATHEN SHOULD RULE OVER THEM: wherefore should they say among the people, Where is their God? (*Joel 2:16-17*)

After true repentance, then the fire of anointing for revival, blessing and power can come. The former and latter rain is loosed on the people, just as the rain was released after the confrontation on Mount Carmel.

1. A sacrifice was offered.
2. The people turned to YHWH and made a declaration of their faith.
3. The people acted on their faith: Together, they and Elijah killed the false prophets.
4. The true prophet, Elijah, prayed fervently, and the rains came; not a few drops but a torrent, a flood.
5. Elijah RAN before the King's chariot.

All who are born again are a royal priesthood according to the Word *(1 Peter 2:9)*, **all** may prophesy *(1 Corinthians 14:39)*, and we must all repent for ourselves, our complacency, and our nation. Then we will see the fulfillment of revival FIRE, a flood of power as on Pentecost *(Acts 2:17)* which was prophesied in Joel.

And it shall come to pass afterward, that I will POUR OUT MY SPIRIT UPON ALL FLESH: and your sons and your daughters shall prophesy, your old men shall dream dreams, your young men shall see visions: And also upon the servants and upon the handmaids in those days will I pour out My Spirit. And I will show wonders in the heavens and in the earth, blood and FIRE, and pillars of smoke. *(Joel 2:28-30)*

The day of the LORD is at hand!

Even now, the forces of darkness are gathering, for they have broken through "the gap," a *real* location where intercession takes place. Only a few have been willing to stand in the gap and fight in the Spirit to save our country. Now is the season for true intercessors: selfless, faceless servants of the Most High, who will not lay down the sword of the Spirit, but will forcefully advance into enemy territory and take back what the devil has stolen. Yahshua Messiah, the Captain of our salvation, will stand with us as we fight the good fight of faith.

The minions of the wicked one are literally gathering like a storm cloud over our nation and our world. There will be another intense conflict between Elijah and Jezebel, whom I believe now has dominion, along with the antichrist spirit, over our nation. Jezebel has successfully established false religions in our country, helped them gain strength and credibility, and polluted the minds of the people.

The proliferation of witchcraft and New Age religions is at epic proportions. One presidential candidate raised funds from a Buddhist temple, and wrote in his book his belief that we should worship nature; the creature rather than the creator. The lewdness, sensuality, and child sacrifice (legalized abortion) of our culture is reminiscent of the ancient pagan fertility cults, Baal and Ashtoreth worship. In a 1998 survey of Promise Keepers, 62% of the men admitted to using pornography weekly, and 40% of pastors confessed to committing adultery. Yes, Baal worship is alive and well in our country.

In the days of the prophet Samuel, he told the people to put away their pagan gods and YHWH would save them from the hand of the Philistines. Remember that Ashtoreth worship included rampant sexual sin, homosexuality, infant sacrifice, bowing down to avarice, lying, whoredoms, greed and vice. Sounds like America today!

And Samuel spake unto all the house of Israel, If ye do return unto the LORD, with all your hearts, then PUT AWAY THE STRANGE GODS AND AS-TORETH from among you, and PREPARE YOUR HEARTS UNTO THE LORD, and serve Him only: and HE WILL DELIVER YOU out of the hand of the Philistines. (*1 Samuel 7:3*)

The people repented and fasted on the top of Mount Mizpeh.

And they gathered together to Mizpeh, and drew water, and poured it out before the LORD, and FASTED on that day, and said there, WE HAVE SINNED against the LORD. And Samuel JUDGED the children of Israel, in Mizpeh. (*1 Samuel 7:6*)

While this was taking place the Philistines, thinking the Israelites were vulnerable when seeking YHWH in prayer, gathered against them. They didn't know that this was the time when YHWH's followers are the most invincible: *When on their knees.*

And Samuel took a sucking lamb, and offered it for a burnt offering wholly unto the LORD: and Samuel cried unto the LORD for Israel; and the LORD heard him. (*1 Samuel 7:9*)

This was yet another showdown, as YHWH defeated His enemies, showing Himself strong when the people repented and the prophets prayed.

And as Samuel was offering up the burnt offering, the Philistines drew near in battle against Israel: but the LORD THUNDERED WITH A GREAT THUNDER on that day upon the Philistines, and DISCOMFITED them; and they were SMITTEN before Israel. (*1 Samuel 7:10*)

According to *Strong's* the word THUNDER, ra'am, means to tumble with violent agitation, to crash, roar, to trouble. The word DISCOMFITED, huwm, means to make an uproar, agitate greatly, destroy, move, make a noise. SMITTEN, nagaph, means to push, gore, defeat, inflict, beat, dash, hurt, plague, slay, smite, strike.

Our God was willing to do **all that and more** to the enemies of Israel when Israel humbled themselves and:

1. Repented (turned from their sin and idol worship).
2. Fasted (openly demonstrated a contrite heart through giving up food, a pleasure of the flesh).
3. Fervently sought his face (intense prayer time).
4. Allowed their sin to be *judged* (allowed the prophet to bring conviction and judgment for their sins——today the Holy Spirit will speak to us directly, or through a prophet or preacher).
5. Sacrificed a "lamb" for their sins (symbolic of Yahshua Messiah's sacrifice of the cross—only through the shedding of blood can there be remission of sins—Yahshua, our Passover Lamb, did this once for all of us).
6. Fervently prayed for deliverance from enemies (the LORD hears and delivers).

If I shut up the heaven that there be no RAIN...If my people, which are called by My Name, shall humble themselves, and pray, and seek My face, and turn from their wicked ways; then will I hear from heaven, and will forgive their sin, and will heal their land. NOW Mine eyes shall be open, and Mine ears attent unto the prayer that is made in this place. (*2 Chronicles 7:13-15*)

Elijah	Jezebel
Withstood Jezebel	Threatened Elijah
Exposed her sin	Never repented
John exposed Herodias	She had him killed
Fear came in to Elijah and to John	To the unprepared today Jezebel inspires fear & makes her victims weak

True prophecies	False prophets & prophecies
Visions & dreams	Excessive false visions & dreams
Turns hearts of fathers to children	Turns hearts to idols & lusts of the flesh
We are living in former and latter rain	Quenching of the Spirit
Elijah will again call fire down from heaven	Lying signs and wonders
True prophets must arise and take proper authority	Jezebel takes authority anywhere she can
Spirit of prophecy is revelation of Yahshua Messiah (Jesus Christ)	Revelation of antichrist / of Satan
Yahshua is the light of the world	Comes as angel of light/ to deceive/ comes like a minister
True prophets manifest fruit of spirit/ judge the fruit/ discern fruit	Satan masquerades as true prophet/even the elect will be deceived

Part Six

The End Of
This Age

Fear none of those things which thou shalt suffer: behold, the devil shall cast some of you into prison, that ye may be tried...be thou faithful unto death, and I will give thee a crown of life. *Revelation 2:10*

39

Types and Shadows of the Forerunner Spirit

The final clash of spirits and the battle in the heavenlies is upon us. There were several Old Testament deliverers both men and women, whom YHWH raised up to lead His people in times of crisis. We can study their lives for keys to the battle in such a time as this. We will march in the dunamis power of YHWH with arms linked, fully armored, declaring that the battle is the LORD's but the victory is ours. This end-time move of the Spirit was foreshadowed time and again in the Bible.

Moses

Moses, the deliverer, was born in a time of great slaughter of infant boys, and raised up out of a baptism of water to grow up in a king's palace, only to find himself forty years on the backside of the desert. His rash passion for justice was tempered over time as he was patiently tried in the wilderness. Then a day came when the "I Am" appeared to him in a burning bush. He learned through obedience the ways of YHWH, but he had a burning desire to see His face. This sublime passion for the presence of God kept him in all the tests but one. The old temper flared up over the people's disobedience. He should have let YHWH handle things His way, but instead Moses disobeyed a specific command. For this he could not enter the promised land. We must set the course of our hearts for the purpose and plan of YHWH, never allowing our flesh to interfere.

Joseph

Joseph, interpreter of dreams, was God's man of the hour, placed strategically in Egypt by divine plan, to save the seed of Abraham, the friend of God. I'm sure he didn't enjoy the method by which he arrived in this position, yet he never complained or lost hope. He was thrown in a pit, falsely accused, unjustly tossed into Pharaoh's prison, and made to wait for years in a seemingly hopeless situation, yet he brought honor to God through his impeccable character, honesty and because he used his gifts to glorify God.

He learned patience through his trials. Even the dreams he interpreted in prison had significance for us today, as a type and shadow. The decoding of these dreams eventually set him free from prison. The bread maker was killed symbolizing Yahshua Messiah's body which suffered death, but the wine taster lived, symbolizing that there is new life in the blood. We must crucify the flesh daily, for we are given life through the shed blood of our Savior.

Whether in feast or famine, YHWH will provide for His faithful ones and see us through the tests, tried as gold. There may be a sojourn in the land of Egypt but a deliverer has come to lift us out of bondage. Joseph was a type and shadow of Jesus. He delivered his people, the seed of Abraham, when he saved Egypt's grain for bread. Jesus, as the promised deliverer of the seed of Abraham, was the bread of life through whom we are all saved. Joseph's bones were preserved and carried into the promised land unbroken. Jesus' bones were also unbroken in death. We will be raised up to sit together in heavenly places with our Savior in unbreakable fellowship, according to His great and precious promises. Joseph learned patience through his trials and in the end he triumphed because he never lost sight of the heavenly vision.

Esther

Esther, a type of the bride of Christ, was a deliverer to her people, placed strategically by God to save the Jews. After the death of her parents she was raised by her guardian, Mordecai. She was selected to become royalty in a pagan nation, as were Joseph and Moses before her. Though inexperienced, she relied totally on the power of YHWH to save her and her people. She was tried through a baptism of fire, as she fasted and prayed fervently for

God to move in her behalf, and took her life in her hands to stand before the king. He raised the golden septor to her, saving her from instant death, and empowered her to deliver God's people from the senseless slaughter planned for them. Through total reliance on YHWH for wisdom and protection, she revealed the beauty of the bride that we are to be.

John the Baptist

John the Baptist had the forerunner spirit; the Elijah spirit. He was a voice of one crying in the wilderness. Born in the time of Herod's great slaughter of infants, he was the greatest of God's prophets, blessed with the task of introducing and making the paths straight for the people to receive the Messiah. He was tried both in the wilderness and in Herod's prison. He learned obedience through hardship and died for speaking the truth regardless of the consequences.

Yahshua (Jesus)

Yahshua, the greatest deliverer of all and Son of YHWH, was born in a lowly stable. Following his birth there was a great slaughter of infants, as in the days of Moses. After a baptism in water He was tested in the wilderness, but unlike Moses, He overcame fleshly trials, victorious over the temptations of the devil, and crushed Satan under His heel. He arose from the grave triumphant, set the captives free and entered into His promise, a conquering hero. Though Moses, a type and shadow of Jesus, could not enter the promised land because of sin, we, through Jesus' perfect blood, can enter into His great and precious promises.

The forerunner spirit

The Elijah's are running before the king's chariot again, rejoicing, *for "our" King is holy,* and has overcome the sins of the flesh. He has enabled us to hide in the safety of His presence. The great slaughter of infants began in America in 1973, as it did in Moses' and Yahshua's time, increasing exponentially with the idolatry and greed of the people. Persecution of Christians in this country and around the world has escalated to astounding proportions, but we have turned a blind eye.

The corrupt and degenerate behavior of the leaders of our nation and its people is exploding, juxtaposed against the equal but opposite lukewarm condition of Christians who turn blind eyes to their leader's wickedness. Elijah, John the Baptist, and Yahshua stood up to their immoral leaders and exposed their sin. The end-time soldiers of God will do the same!

Baptism of fire

As the baptism of fire increases for the righteous, they will be tried again and again in the wilderness of the temptations of the flesh. Some will be thrown into prison, some will be killed for their beliefs and all will endure trials. Temper and disobediance will be burned out by holy fire. True believers will turn from sin to fast and pray, laying their lives at the feet of their King.

Brothers and sisters throughout the world are standing up for the Name of Yahshua (Jesus), suffering persecution and death for their faith. We will learn obedience as the men and women of old did. We will overcome the wicked spirit of this age by the blood of the Lamb, the word of our testimony, and love not our lives unto death. *(Revelation 12:11)* Then we will enter into the promised land of the LORD.

40
The End of
the Age

The events at the end of the age are clearly spelled out for us in the book of Revelation. Jezebel keeps turning up like a bad penny, her licentious character still at work in the hearts of men. Woe unto all who allow Jezebel to operate, or who follow her schemes. The fear of YHWH should come on all God's people who read the following passage of scripture.

> **I have a few things against thee, because thou suf-ferest that woman Jezebel, which calleth herself a prophetess, to teach and to seduce my servants to commit fornication, and to eat things sacrificed unto idols. And I GAVE HER SPACE TO REPENT of her FORNICATION; and she repented not. Behold, I will cast her into a bed, and THEM THAT COMMIT ADULTERY WITH HER INTO GREAT TRIBU-LATION, except they repent of their deeds. And I will kill her children with death; and ALL the churches shall know that I am He which searcheth the reins and hearts: and I will give unto every one of you according to your works. But unto you I say... as many as have not this doctrine, and which have not known the depths of Satan, as they speak; I will put upon you none other burden. But that which ye have already hold fast till I come. And he that overcometh, and keepeth my works unto the END, to him will I give power over the nations...** *(Revelation 2:20-26)*

"Fornication" in this context also means idolatry. This is a very serious warning.

Things YHWH says about Jezebel

1. She calls herself a prophetess. She is a false prophet.
2. She teaches idolatry. She twists the truth in order to deceive, gain possessions and followers.
3. She seduces God's servants into committing fornication. Never be so arrogant in your walk with God that you think yourself impervious to temptation. This scripture clearly states that she *does* succeed, seducing some of God's servants.
4. She entices them to eat things sacrificed to idols.
5. She was given space to repent. God is merciful, slow to anger, for he desires that none should perish.
6. She refused to repent. Notice Jezebel does *not* repent!
7. She will be cast into a bed of wickedness, fornication, adultery, and idolatry.
8. Those who follow her will also be cast into the same bed with her unless they repent.
9. Her followers will be cast into **great tribulation.**
10. God will kill her children with death (those who follow her). This means *eternal* death.
11. All the congregations will realize that YHWH is sovereign.
12. We must remember that God searches the hearts of us all.
13. We will all receive our true rewards according to our works.
14. If we have not succumbed to the depths of Satan, as Jezebel did, our Father will put on us no other burden.
15. God commands us to hold fast, standing against the devil and all his wiles, until Yahshua (Jesus) comes again.
16. We must be overcomers.
17. We must keep God's works until the end.
18. If we overcome and keep His works until the *end*, He will give us power over the nations.

Snare of the fowler

Several years ago I was praying about a situation concerning one of God's servants. He was thinking about joining with a certain minister to start an outreach ministry. I saw a vision of a beautiful woman floating toward him with outstretched arms, beckoning him to follow in a seductive way. I know now that this was a warning not to follow this minister, for he turned out later to have a Jezebel spirit.

The deal appeared enticing, just what he was looking for, but it was a trap of the enemy to destroy his credibility and ministry. He would have had to sell his home and move into a building in another city to work with this ministry. All the money from selling his house would have been seduced away from him by Jezebel, and his family would have been left destitute.

As it was, the man with the Jezebel spirit lost the building he was planning to use for the outreach, after enticing dozens of people to invest large amounts. Amazingly, he seemed to retain abundant finances to move and start this same scheme elsewhere. He has been going from town to town ever since, inducing his followers to invest in a ministry he is "going to begin in another city." He has fleeced thousands of people in this manner.

Fear of YHWH only

It is hard to determine the depths of depravity to which Jezebel and her followers sank in ancient times, but it was an abomination to YHWH. Her devotees are still an abomination and will pay a terrible price for following her. YHWH enjoins the church earlier in Revelation:

> **Fear none of those things which thou shalt suffer: behold, the devil shall cast some of you into prison, that ye may be TRIED (tested), and ye shall have tribulation ten days: BE THOU FAITHFUL UNTO DEATH, and I will give thee a crown of life.** (*Revelation 2:10*)

We are not to fear death if we are "righteous" through Jesus' blood. We have been warned that tribulation will come and that we will be **tested**. Let's try to pass this **test**! We may not receive another chance for we are dangerously close to the end of this age.

If we can be faithful unto death, YHWH will give us a crown of life. **Let's live for what is written in heaven!** Our world is headed straight for judgment. **We must not tolerate Jezebel for one more day!** When persecution comes as we expose her and take a stand for righteousness, we can rejoice that our names are written in the Lamb's Book of Life. (*Luke 10:20*)

> **Now is come salvation, and STRENGTH, and the kingdom of our God, and the power of His Christ: for**

the ACCUSER of our brethren is cast down, which
accused them before our God day and night. And they
overcame him by the blood of the Lamb, and by the word
of their testimony; and they LOVED NOT THEIR
LIVES UNTO THE DEATH. *(Revelation 12:10-11)*

Strength and treasure through YHWH

The word STRENGTH in *Revelation 12:10* means treasure, or
treasurer. You have great treasure in the Messiah. Jezebel can only
offer temporal pleasure, the lusts of the flesh, but with Jesus we
have *eternal* treasure. We are earthen vessels which hold the true
treasure, Jesus and His salvation in our hearts.

The word salvation includes our deliverance from danger and
temptation if we will only trust in God with all our hearts and lean
not on our own understanding, in all our ways acknowledge Him
and He will direct our paths. *(Proverbs 3:3-6)*

The accuser works continually through Jezebel

Jezebel had Naboth and his sons accused. She even accused
her accusers, Elijah and Jehu. If you come against Jezebel, she
will come against you with accusations. She may call you or
confront you falsely accusing you by telephone rather than to your
face. Jezebel is really a coward. She will bear false witness against
you behind your back. Now is the time to choose whom you will
serve. Elijah's challenge rings as true for us as it did for the
Israelites of his day.

How long halt ye between two opinions? if the
LORD be God, follow Him: but if Baal, then follow
him. (*1 Kings 18:21*)

How to overcome Jezebel and the accuser

1. We have salvation and strength through Yahshua haMashiach
   (Jesus Christ).
2. We overcome by the blood of the Lamb.
3. We overcome by the word of our testimony.
4. We love *not* our lives unto death.

And they overcame him by the blood of the Lamb,
and by the word of their testimony; and THEY
LOVED NOT THEIR LIVES UNTO THE DEATH.
(*Revelation 12:11*)

A key to defeating Jezebel

You will be *unable* to resist Jezebel if you fear death. Jesus
came to deliver us from "fear of death."

...that through death He might destroy him that had
the power of death, that is, the devil; And deliver them
who through FEAR OF DEATH were all their lifetime
SUBJECT TO BONDAGE. (*Hebrews 2:14-15*)

The word SUBJECT in the above scripture means slave,
danger, guilty, liable, penalty, imputation. If you are a slave to the
fear of death you *are* in mortal danger. Instead, choose to trust
God for your salvation, strength and deliverance, beginning now.
Otherwise, when the chips are down, you will be too busy protecting your own life, trying to save your own reputation, currying
men's favor and fawning all over Jezebel. Yuk!

Therefore rejoice, ye heavens, and ye that dwell in
them. Woe to the inhabiters of earth and of the sea! for
the devil is come down unto you having great wrath,
because he knoweth that he hath but a short time.
(*Revelation 12:12*)

41

Rejection
and
Forgiveness

In chapter one of Hosea, the LORD told Hosea to name his first son Jezreel, meaning "God scatters."

Jezreel = God will sow; God has scattered (represents seed and harvest)
  • Root word of Jezreel is "zara" meaning to sow, bear, conceive seed, fructify, yield

God also said He would avenge the blood of Jezreel upon the house of Jehu, and cause to cease the kingdom of the house of Israel in the valley in Jezreel, the place of Jezebel's ivory palace and Naboth's vineyard.

Hosea's second child was named Loruhamah, meaning rejection, no mercy, reversal of compassion. There came a time for Jezebel and Ahab when judgment arrived. The same thing happened to Israel and it will happen to America, as well.

His third child's name was Loammi, which means "you are not my people and I will not be your God." Israel was carried away into captivity after their refusal to turn from whoring after other gods. The same fate awaits an unrepentant America.

Seed time and harvest

With God, there is always seed time and harvest. Hosea is a type and shadow of our Bridegroom, Jesus, seeking to redeem His faithless bride. Hosea's wife Gomer, who had gone whoring after her idolatrous lovers but found no satisfaction, was redeemed and forgiven, just like our Bridegroom, Jesus, forgives us. God caused Hosea to name his three children as a reflection of His chastening of Israel, to be a sign and a foreshadowing, a witness of

His promise of the coming harvest and eventual redemption of His Bride. Hosea bought Gomer back from bondage and sin she herself caused, and forgave her, just as God bought us back through Jesus' blood, and forgave us.

And I will betroth thee unto Me forever... (*Hosea 2:19*)

YHWH, our God, is redeeming a bride for His Son. He is redeeming a people who are not His people:

> **...I will hear the HEAVENS, and they shall hear the EARTH; And the earth shall hear the CORN, and the WINE, and the OIL; and they shall hear Jezreel. And I will sow her unto me in the earth; and I will have mercy upon her that had not obtained mercy; and I will say to them WHICH WERE NOT MY PEOPLE, Thou art my people; and they shall say, Thou art my God. (*Hosea 2:21-23*)**

CORN, OIL and WINE are all symbols of revival and God's goodness. As we sow to the *heaven*s through our repentance, praises, worship and prayer, YHWH sows to the *earth* blessings, holy fire, revival and redemption. God will have mercy on us and bring repentance to our hearts as we seek His will and presence daily in our lives. The LORD promises that if we press in to know Him and follow Him, there will be both goodness and revival.

> **Then shall we know if we follow on to know the LORD: His going forth is prepared as the morning; and He shall come unto us as the RAIN, as the LATTER AND FORMER RAIN unto the earth. (*Hosea 6:3*)**

Notice the reference again to rain. This is the same rain referred to in Joel 2 and in Acts 2. The rain is the outpouring of YHWH's Spirit that He has longed to release on our generation, the end-time church, as He did in the early church. The difference is that we will have both the former and latter rain. Entreat, with all fervency of spirit, the congregation where you attend, the people you know, to repent and prepare for revival. Those who endure *until the end*, refusing to yield to the schemes of the enemy, or run in fear, will receive a great reward: being with Yahshua Messiah forever.

42

The Bride

Laodicea was a city of banks and wealth. They were noted for making an eyesalve that healed eye disorders. Yet they, themselves, could not see the truth. The Laodiceans represent the present day church and thus are a warning to put on the white garments of Christ's righteousness and see through the eyesalve of the Holy Spirit. The *lukewarm*, compromised state of the church today, and its blind pride, is a stench to our zealous God.

> **And unto the angel of the church of the Laodiceans write; These things saith the Amen, the faithful and true witness, the beginning of the creation of God; I know thy works, that THOU ART NEITHER COLD NOR HOT: I would thou wert cold or hot. So then because thou art LUKEWARM, and neither cold nor hot, I will SPEW thee out of my mouth.**
>
> **Because thou sayest, I am rich, and increased with goods, and have need of nothing; and knowest not that thou art wretched, and miserable, and poor, and blind, and naked...** (*Revelation 3:14-17*)

Think about the nauseating properties of being LUKEWARM. Cold is refreshing, or at least a definite choice. Hot is medicinal, cleansing, fiery with decision. No wonder YHWH wants to vomit (spew) out the Laodicean church. They neither *refresh* nor *heal*, they fail to *come* to Jesus, or *go* into all the world to preach the gospel. They just veg-out.

One of the great deceptions of our time is the wretched state of God's people. As they race through their busy lives believing they are right with YHWH, they are often deceived through pride and self-righteous acceptance of a *lukewarm* existence. The fiery personality of Elijah would *not* fit at their nice social functions. The fear of the LORD does not enter into the competition for their time and attentions. I pray for their slumber to cease! I pray for their hearts to be open to the moving of the Spirit and I pray genuine revival would break out in waves across our land.

The beauty of the bride

Let "The Bride" arise and call upon the Name of her Beloved with renewed passion! Let her clarion call be trumpeted forth to a lost and dying world, and let her beauty shine for all to see. Let white-hot, fervent zeal spring forth in her, that utterly replaces the fence-riding complacent slumber that has been the status-quo. Let the fire of the Holy Spirit (Ruach haKodesh—the set-apart Spirit) cleanse and prepare her to stand before a Holy God.

And the Spirit and the bride say, Come. And let him that heareth say, Come. And let him that is athirst come. And whosoever will, let him take the water of life freely. (*Revelation 22:17*)

YHWH's remnant wears whole armor of God

The bride wears the belt of truth, the shoes of peace, the helmet of salvation, the breastplate of righteousness, the shield of faith, and she takes up the sword of the Spirit. In holiness before the Father, she will not compromise nor look the other way in apathy where wickedness abounds, nor will she flinch from the persecution that is *sure* to come.

She will hold her standard high and her plumb line of right and wrong will be measured in the light of the glorious gospel of Yahshua Messiah. Though the enemy comes in like a flood, the banner of her God, YHWH, and His Son, Yahshua, will be lifted high.

She will never be defeated for she has no fear of death, therefore death cannot hold her. She wears the mantle of humility, the cloak of zeal and the garment of vengeance. In her right hand she carries truth, and in her left hand she bears wisdom and understanding. Above all, she walks in love, abounding in the fruit of the spirit (love, joy, peace, longsuffering, gentleness, goodness, faith, meekness and temperance).

...let everyone come who is thirsty [who is painfully aware and conscious of his need of those things by

which the soul is REFRESHED, SUPPORTED,   and STRENGTHENED; and whoever [earnestly] desires to do it, let him come, take, appropriate, and DRINK THE WATER OF LIFE without cost. (*Revelation 22:17 Amplified*)

She abides in the shadow of the Almighty, for the LORD is her refuge and her fortress. She wears the garment of praise through *all* life's circumstances for the joy of the LORD is her strength. She is strong and does great exploits for she knows her God. She will overcome the wicked one by the blood of the Lamb and the word of her testimony, and she will love not her life unto death.

He which testifieth these things saith, Surely
I come quickly. Amen.
Even so, come, LORD Jesus.
Revelation 22:20

Bibliography

1. Drummelow, *The One Volume Bible Commentary*, p. 17.1
2. *The New Schaff-Herzog Encyc. of Religious Know.*, p. 392
3. Gray, *Near Eastern Mythology*, p. 81
4. *Abington Bible Commentary*, p.426
5. Ibid., p. 313-314
6. *Smith's Bible Dictionary*, p.119
7. Ibid., p.162
8. *Smith's Bible Handbook*, p.206
9. *The Interpreter's Dictionary of the Bible*, Vol.1, p. 328-329
10. *The New Schaff-Herzog Encyc. of Religious Know.*, p. 392
11. *Smith's Bible Dictionary*, p.166, 198
12. *The Interpreter's Dictionary of the Bible*, Vol.1 p.167
13. *Smith's Bible Dictionary*, p.119
14. *The Two Babylons*, pp.24-27
15. Ibid. p.44-45
16. Ibid. p.21
17. Ibid. p.103-110
18. Ibid.
19. Ibid. p. 21
20. Ibid. p.103-110
21. Ibid. p.21
22. Ibid.
23. *The Broadman Bible Commentary*, p. 251
24. Ibid.
25. Ibid.
26. Bacon, "Prophetic Training Course," Level 2, 1997
27. *Smith's Bible Handbook*, p.199
28. *Smith's Bible Dictionary*, p. 256
29. Croft, *The Jezebel Influence*, p.1-11
30. Binyamin Baruch, *The Day of the LORD*, p.248
31. Ibid., p.249
32. Ibid., p.55
33. Ibid.
34. *The Occult in Your Living Room*, video by Stephen Dollins
35. Ibid.
36. Ibid.

194   Bree M. Keyton

37. Ibid.
38. Ibid.
39. Ibid.
40. Ibid.
41. Ibid.
42. Ibid.
43. Ibid.
44. Ibid.
45. Ibid.
46. Ibid.
47. Ibid.
48. Ibid.
49. Ibid.
50. *The Interpreters Dictionary*, p.422
51. "The Ancient Paths," cassette by Craig Hill
52. Larson, *The American Republic*, p.57-59
53. "The Ancient Paths," cassette by Craig Hill
54. Lockyer, *All the Women of the Bible*, p.73
55. Frangipane, *The Jezebel Spirit*, p.17-18
56. Frangipane, *The Jezebel Spirit*, p.20
57. Bell, *The Ahab Spirit*

Worshipping Warriors Fellowship
an affiliation of Bree Keyton Ministries
Order online: www.breekeytonministries.com

Catalog

BOOKS
1. Stripes, Nails, Thorns & The Blood $25.00
2. Jezebel vs. Elijah $14.00
3. The Passion: What Does It Mean? $14.00

DVDs
1. Jezebel vs. Elijah $25.00
2. Spiritual Weapons of Our Warfare $25.00
3. The Passion & the Passover $25.00
4. Extreme Spiritual Warfare $30.00

SCRIPTURE STAKE
Stake $10.00 (wooden)

MUSIC
Heart & Soul Surrender (music)
($16 CD - $13 Cassette)

TEACHING / MINISTRY
1. Advanced Spiritual Warfare $50.00 (twelve CDs)
2. Healing Scriptures $14.00 (2 CDs)
3. Bitter-Root Judgments $12.00 (CD)
4. Victorious Scriptures $14.00 (2 CDs)
5. Freemasonry $14.00 (2 CDs)
6. Twenty-Three Minutes in Hell $5.00 (CD)
7. How to Survive the Last Days! $20.00 (2 CDs)

Chapter 1
Study Questions

1. Why did YHWH send Elijah to the people of Israel?
2. For how long did Elijah declare it would not rain?
3. Where was Jezebel from, originally? Find it on a map?
4. Give several reasons why you think Ahab wanted to marry Jezebel?
5. Why was he willing to begin worshiping her gods?
6. Who was Jezebel's father?
7. What is the significance of his name?
8. Was Israel the Northern or Southern Kingdom?
9. How many of the original twelve tribes lived in Israel?
10. What kind of palace did Jezebel live in?
11. Is the Jezebel spirit the same today as it was in 800 B.C?
12. How did Baal's prophets behave during the contest?
13. What kind of god did Baal's worshippers believe him to be?
14. Ultimately, who won the contest?
15. How did YHWH prove He is "THE" God?
16. What was done to Baal's prophets?

Reading Assignment

Read all of 1 Kings chapter 16. This chapter will provide background for subsequent reading assignments.

Chapter 2
Study Questions

1. How is Jezebel ruling and reigning in people's hearts today?
2. What does the expression "wag the dog" mean?
3. What was the lifestyle of the Israelites during Jezebel's reign?
4. Why did Elijah run in fear?
5. Did the same wicked spirit of Jezebel attack John the Baptist?
6. How could this happen?
7. Do you believe Elijah is coming back?
8. Look at Revelation 3, verses 5, 6, and 11.
   a. What similarities do you see between each of these scriptures and the chapter in this book that you just read?

Reading Assignment

Read Joel 2:28-32 and 3:1-21. Notice the reference to Zidon in verse 3:4.

Read Revelation 11:3-12.
Read Malachi 4:6 and Luke 1:17.

Chapter 3
Study Questions

1. What spirit is behind the corruption in our government and media?
2. How do you know this? Be specific.
3. How did YHWH protect Elijah?
   a. List three ways.
   b. Link these ways with YHWH's provision.
4. How will YHWH watch over you in times of trouble?
5. What does the word "much" mean in James 5:16?
6. How does Jezebel lull us into sin?
7. What does she do then?
8. What are some things that Jezebel likes to control?
9. What is the spirit of slumber?
10. How does it operate?
11. What did Elijah call people to?
12. What can you do personally to help rid the church of Jezebel?
13. Are you willing to stand up and proclaim the truth?
14. Are you fearful of Jezebel?
    a. Find scriptures to stand on to overcome fear.
    b. Memorize them.

Reading Assignment

Read 1 Kings 17.

Chapter 4
Study Questions

1. What happens when a person stands against Jezebel?
2. What action should be taken?
3. Give scriptures to back this up.
4. Is it acceptable to retaliate against the *person* who is your accuser?
5. Who should you retaliate against?
6. Give some strategies you have learned from this chapter for prayer against Jezebel.

Reading Assignment

Read 1 Kings 18.

Chapter 5
Study Questions

1. What is Jezebel's favorite stomping ground?
2. How long has it been since the flesh and blood Jezebel lived?
3. What spirit is arising now, in our time, to combat Jezebel?
4. Who was the forerunner of Jesus the Messiah that announced His coming?
5. What spirit was on this man?
6. What kind of god was Baal?
7. What was he worshipped for?
8. What did Jezebel do to the prophets of YHWH?

Reading Assignment

Read 1 Kings 18:1-14.
Read Deuteronomy 28:12.
Read Deuteronomy 1:17.

Chapter 6
Study Questions

1. What was the issue to be settled between YHWH and Baal?
2. What does YHWH prove?
3. What was the question in the people's minds?
4. What is the deception Satan perpetrates against the true prophets?
5. How many false prophets were gathered against YHWH?
6. Why don't the people speak when Elijah questions them? (Verse 18:21)
7. What does the word "halt" mean?
8. Do you know anyone who wavers between serving the true God and following their own course?
9. Is Elijah the only prophet left in Israel?
10. Are we ever alone when we stand against wickedness?
11. By what method does Elijah expect YHWH to answer the challenge?
12. How does Elijah treat Baal's prophets?
13. How do they respond?
14. How long did Baal's prophets spend trying to get Baal to respond?
15. What may have been some of their reasons for their wild behavior?

Reading Assignment

Read 1 Kings 18:15-28.

Chapter 7
Study Questions

1. Notice the Baal prophets prophesied, too. What do you think they were saying?
2. Did their god answer them?
3. Why does Elijah draw the people near to him?
4. Why does Elijah use "12" stones for the sacrifice?
5. Why does he have them fill buckets twelve times with water?
6. What time was the evening sacrifice?
7. How did Elijah pray?
8. How did YHWH answer?
9. What was the people's response?
10. What does Elijah do to Baal's prophets?
11. Why does Elijah encourage Ahab?
12. What does Elijah mean when he says he hears the *sound* of rain?

Reading Assignment

Read 1 Kings 18:30-41.
Read Deuteronomy 13:5

Chapter 8
Study Questions

1. How is it possible to rise so high in victory and then fall so far into despair, as Elijah did?
2. Why did Ahab run to Jezebel with the news of Baal's defeat?
3. How did she respond?
4. Why does Elijah run in fear?
5. Why does he run so far away?
6. Why does Elijah say he's not better than his fathers?
7. Why does YHWH show Elijah the fire, the earthquake and the whirlwind?
8. How does YHWH finally speak to Elijah?
9. What does YHWH tell Elijah?

Reading Assignment

Read 1 Kings 19.

Chapter 9
Study Questions

1. How does Jezebel view herself?
2. How does she regard YHWH's laws?
3. Who lives in Jezreel?
4. For what purpose does Ahab want Naboth's vineyard?
5. Why is this wrong?
6. How does YHWH view Naboth and his vineyard?
7. What does Ahab do when Naboth turns down his offer to buy the vineyard?
8. In what way does Jezebel take advantage of the situation?

Reading Assignment

Read 1 Kings 21:1-7

Chapter 10
Study Questions

1. What is idolatry?
2. What was Ashtoreth worshipped for?
3. What were her attributes believed to be?
4. Who introduced Baal and Ashtoreth worship to the Israelites?
5. How many Israelites were in Israel when Jezebel became queen?
6. What position did Jezebel's father hold in addition to being king?
7. How would this have affected his daughter, Jezebel?
8. Where were the first pagan rituals observed?
9. Why were the Israelite people so easily led into Baal worship ?
10. What was Ahab's greatest crime according to scripture?
11. What significance does the struggle between Jezebel and Elijah have, both then and now?
12. For what attributes was Baal worshiped?
13. Why do you think the worship of these false gods was so appealing to the Israelites?

Reading Assignment

Read Ezekiel chapters 8 and 9

Chapter 11
Study Questions

1. Under whose leadership was language confounded?
2. Whose son was he and who was his wife?
3. Who was the son of the confounder and who was his wife?
4. What happened to Nimrod?
5. How were the mystery religions begun?
6. What are three names for Nimrod that you recognize from the list?
7. What are three names for Semiramis that you recognize from the list?
8. What is the "weeping" for, referred to in Ezekiel?
9. What ancient pagan practices still exist today from this "weeping?"
10. What is the origin of today's Easter holiday?
11. What is the origin of today's Christmas holiday?
12. Who was the first deified woman?

Reading Assignment

Read Deuteronomy 27:15-26; 28:9-14.
Read Leviticus 18:13-23; 20:6, 27.
Read Genesis 10:1-10.
Read 1 Chronicles 1:10.
Read Micah 5:6.

Chapter 12
Study Questions

1. What kind of character does Jezebel have?
2. How does she accomplish the destruction of Naboth and his sons?
3. Did Ahab know what she was doing?
4. Why didn't he stop her?
5. How does this story show the unscrupulous nature of Jezebel?

6. How did Jezebel usurp the kingdom through this incident?
7. How did Ahab behave after Naboth's murder?
8. Was it really Naboth's vineyard that Jezebel was after?
9. Who is Belial?
10. Why is it amazing in Israel's culture that the men do Jezebel's bidding?
11. What were the legal customs that Jezebel used to her advantage?
12. How does Jezebel regard others?
13. Why did Jezebel need to destroy Naboth's sons?

Reading Assignment

Read 1 Kings 21:1-16.
Read 2 Kings 9:26.

Chapter 13
Study Questions

1. What did Elijah say to Ahab when he tried to possess the vineyard?
2. How long did Jezebel live after Ahab's death?
3. Who finally defeated Jezebel?
4. What kind of man was he?
5. What was done to Jezebel?
6. Who betrayed her?
7. Do you think she deserved to die the way she did?
8. What was the prophecy spoken against Ahab?
9. In what way does Ahab refer to Elijah?
10. Is this the correct view of YHWH's prophets?
11. Why do you think Ahab felt this way about Elijah?
12. What does Ahab do when he hears the prophecy of doom against him?
13. How does YHWH deal with him?
14. In what way had Ahab sold himself?
15. How is Ahab's repentance like Nineveh's repentance?
16. What was the prophecy against Jezebel?
17. How did Jezebel "stir up" Ahab?

Reading Assignments

Read 1 Kings 21:17-29.
Read Jonah chapters 3 and 4.

Chapter 14
Study Questions

1. What are the differences between man's prophets and YHWH's prophets? List at least three.
2. How did the godly Jehoshaphat get tangled up in an alliance with the wicked Ahab?
3. Does Jehoshaphat believe Ahab's prophets?
4. Who is Micaiah?
5. What is his prophecy to Ahab?
6. How does the messenger try to influence Micaiah?
7. How is he willing to back up his prophecy?
8. Does Ahab believe Micaiah? Does Jehoshaphat?
9. Is Zedekiah man's prophet or YHWH's prophet?
10. Is Micaiah man's prophet or YHWH's?
11. What does Ahab do to Micaiah?
12. What does Zedekiah do to Micaiah?
13. Does Micaiah's prophecy come to pass?
14. Was Ahab's death accidental?
15. What is Ahab's end?

Reading Assignment

Read 1 Kings 22:1-40

Chapter 15
Study Questions

1. What is a revenger of blood?
2. How does Jehu fill that description?
3. What kind of person is Jehu?
4. Who anointed him to be king?
5. How did Jehu approach Jezreel?
6. When asked whether he came in peace, what was his reply?
7. How many kings did he kill in one night?
8. Who did he kill?
9. How did they die?
10. What was done with Joram's body?

Reading Assignment

Read 2 Kings 9:1-29

Chapter 16
Study Questions

1. Who are Jezebel's eunuchs?
2. How did Jezebel behave when Jehu came to her palace?
3. What strategy did she attempt on Jehu?
4. Why does she refer to Zimri?
5. Who turns against Jezebel from among her own servants?
6. What does Jehu tell them to do?
7. Why does Jehu eat and drink after destroying Jezebel?
8. What parts were left of Jezebel?
9. Why are only these parts left?
10. What does this mean symbolically?
11. What is done with these parts?
12. What becomes of Ahab's sons?
13. How many are there?
14. Do you believe it was right to kill all of Ahab's sons?
15. How do you like the person, Jehu?
16. Do you think he is suited to the task he is called to do? Why?

Reading Assignment

Read 2 Kings 9:30-37.

Chapter 17
Study Questions

1. How does Jezebel manifest herself in our time?
2. What does Jezebel call herself?
3. According to Revelation, what will happen to those who tolerate her and sin with her?
4. What is this sin called?
5. Why does YHWH refer to it this way?
6. What spirits combine to make the Jezebel spirit?
7. How does the Jezebel spirit affect those around it?

Reading Assignment

Read Revelation 2:18-29

Chapter 18
Study Questions

1. What evidence of Ahab's ivory palace has been found?
2. Does Jezebel mingle with the common people? Why or why not?
3. In what way does Jezebel "stir up" her victims?
4. What does the word "stirred" (cuwth) mean?
5. What kind of slavery do Jezebel's victims wind up in?
6. Describe some of Jezebel's attributes?
7. What is it like to live with Jezebel?
8. What does Jezebel use in order to control?
9. How does Jezebel know what is going on when she is not there?
10. Can the Jezebel spirit inhabit a man?
11. Why are some people attracted to Jezebel?
12. What do they receive in return?
13. Why does Jezebel feel the need to dominate?
14. How is she a predator?
15. On whom does she prey?
16. How does she rule through perversion and sexual control?
17. Do you know anyone with a Jezebel spirit?
18. How is someone with a Jezebel spirit likely to act when being ministered to?

Reading Assignment

Read 1 Kings 20

Chapter 19
Study Questions

1. Who was the first female persecutor in history?
2. Who is Jezebel's true enemy?
3. What are several things that Jezebel hates? Why?
4. What will the true prophets lead people in?
5. Why is Jezebel fearful of true prophets?
6. How does she silence them?
7. What reactions does she elicit in YHWH's prophets?
8. Why do her prophecies center around "big successes" for those she/he is prophesying to?
9. What methods does Jezebel use to manipulate?
10. What should you do to defend yourself against Jezebel's attacks?

206 Bree M. Keyton

11. What scriptures can you stand on?
12. In what way is Jezebel "man's" prophet?
13. Why are Jezebel's victims flattered by her/him?
14. Why are some of Jezebel's prophecies true?
15. What is mixture in a prophet or ministry leader?
16. What are "show biz" prophets?
17. How is Jezebel a wolf in sheep's clothing?
18. Explain the word "ravening" and how it applies to Jezebel?
19. Why does Jezebel gravitate toward exhibitionism?

Reading Assignment

Read 2 Timothy chapters 3 and 4

Chapter 20
Study Questions

1. Why does Jezebel want to control the money?
2. Why do you think Jezebel often waits to show her true colors?
3. Explain how Jezebel "lies in wait" and "deceives."
4. Discuss how the spirit of exhibitionism operates through Jezebel.
5. In what way does vanity and idolatry play a part in the Jezebel spirit?
6. How does the devil lure show-biz people back into the world, having once served the true God?
7. Why do you think the Jezebel influence is strong on those in the arts and entertainment field?
8. What evidence of this do you see?

Reading Assignment

Read 1 Peter 2:11-12.
Read James 1:13-15.
Read Titus 2:11-14.

Chapter 21
Study Questions

1. What did you learn from reading this chapter?
2. Why is Jezebel's agenda to promote porn?

3. How does she accomplish this?
4. Explain how the spirit of slumber has entered into our nation's mind set?
5. Why do people run after other gods?
6. Is it possible to turn your city around for YHWH?
7. What is meant by "force" and "violence" in Matthew 11:12?
8. How and why is Jezebel involved in gay rights?
9. How does one become a prisoner of Jezebel?
10. In what way does Jezebel wear a mask of submissive behavior?

Reading Assignment

Read James 1.
Read Revelation 1.

Chapter 22
Study Questions

1. What are some parallels between ancient Rome and the USA?
2. What were some of the reasons for Rome's downfall?
3. Why do you think our world is currently being referred to as a global village?
4. What is our only hope?
5. What other nations can you think of that were saved through true repentance?
6. Can you think of a time in your own life when repentance brought God's mercy to you? Describe this event.
7. Why did Yahshua cry during His entrance into Jerusalem?
8. What can you do personally to prepare yourself and others for revival?

Reading Assignment

Read Matthew chapters 24 and 25.
Read Revelation 3.

Chapter 23
Study Questions

1. What are some reasons America will be judged?
2. What does the word "forbear" mean in Proverbs 24:11?
3. How did the president drop the ball on the partial-birth abortion bill?
4. How is this similar to the times when Ahab dropped the ball?
5. Why is abortion an important part of Jezebel's agenda?
6. How does YHWH regard the prayers of those with innocent blood on their hands?
7. What are some of the problems children of Jezebelian parents have?
8. What happens when a nation opens itself up to the same wickedness as the god Molech, slaughtering infants both pre-born and partially born?

Reading Assignment

Read 2 Thessalonians.

Chapter 24
Study Questions

1. What are some of Jezebel's strongest avenues to reach children today?
2. What can parents do to combat the flood of occult information in children's games?
3. What do you think about the Pokemon game and cards?
4. What did you learn about some of the games being manufactured for our children?
5. Were you aware of the content of the games that helped incite the mass murders in schools?

Reading Assignment

Read Jude.
Read Revelation 1.

Chapter 25
Study Questions

1. Name some of Jezebel's predecessors and successors.
2. In what ways are Jezebel and Delilah alike?
3. What is the true source of any man's power?
4. How are Delilah, Jezebel and Athaliah's deaths alike?
5. How are Ahab, Herod and Samson's stories similar?
6. What is YHWH's warning for those who follow their carnal lusts?
7. How did Samson die? Ahab? Jezebel? Delilah?
8. What became of Athaliah?
9. How does Jezebel cause men to doubt their convictions?
10. What similar weaknesses did Herod and Ahab exhibit?
11. How did the Jezebel spirit get John the Baptist to doubt?
12. Why was Athaliah more wicked than her mother?
13. How long did she reign?
14. How did Jehoram do as king of Judah with Athaliah as his wife?
15. What do modern day husbands do when they allow Jezebel to rule in their homes?
16. How did Athaliah's son, Ahaziah, fare as king under her tutelage?

Reading Assignment

Read 1 John 3.
Read 2 Kings 11.

Chapter 26
Study Questions

1. Who is Max Jukes?
2. What kind of a man was he?
3. Who is Jonathan Edwards?
4. What kind of man was he?
5. Name three things that are different about these two men.
6. How do generational blessings and curses affect us?
7. What can we do about these curses?

Reading Assignment

Read Deuteronomy 27:15-26 and 28:1-68.

Chapter 27
Study Questions

1. What are some basic differences between the controlling spirit and the Jezebel spirit?
2. Who may have a controlling spirit?
3. What are some examples of people with controlling spirits?
4. What other spirits operate with the controlling spirit?
5. How does the controlling spirit manifest?
6. Can a person with a controlling spirit be brought to repentance?

Reading Assignment
Read Philippians 2.
Read 1 Timothy 3.

Chapter 28
Study Questions

1. What is Jezebel's worst nightmare?
2. What will a true servant of YHWH manifest?
3. What steps do you need to take to prepare for warring against Jezebel?
4. Why is this important?
5. How can we remove our armor?
6. What does it mean to present your body a living sacrifice?
7. How is this relevant in the war against Jezebel?
8. What does it mean to "stand?"
9. What is the key to defeating Jezebel?

Reading Assignment
Read Romans 12.

Chapter 29
Study Questions

1. What does God's fire do?
2. How will those who stand up against Jezebel be treated?
3. Is it urgent to stand up against Jezebel now? Why?
4. What will happen to Jezebel's followers?
5. What must leaders do to combat Jezebel?

Reading Assignment

Read Revelation 2.

Chapter 33
Study Questions

1. What does Ahab's name mean?
2. Why is this significant?
3. How does a king's (or leader's) wickedness affect the whole nation?
4. How does that apply to our own country?
5. What was Ahab's greatest sin?
6. Who is held responsible for the sin of Baal worship: Jezebel or Ahab?
7. What kind of man was Ahab?
8. Can Jezebel operate by herself?
9. If Jezebel is operating in or through the pastor, who becomes the Ahab?
10. Where does Jezebel like to hide in churches?
11. Why is this?
12. Do you know of any leaders who have succumbed to the seductions of Jezebel?
13. What are some steps to take to avoid this happening to you?

Reading Assignment

Read Revelation chapters 4 and 5.

Chapter 34
Study Questions

1. How can you spot an Ahab?
2. What was the golden opportunity Ahab missed?
3. Who did YHWH send to confront Ahab?
4. Why is Ahab so weak in character?
5. What is the difference between Ahab and David's repentance?
6. What does disorder in the home bring?

Reading Assignment

Read Revelation chapters 6 and 7.

Chapter 35
Study Questions

1. Who protected and fed Elijah during the drought?
2. Who protects you?
3. What is wilderness training?
4. Why do you think it's necessary?
5. Have you had a wilderness experience?
6. Describe what happened?
7. What did it take to wake the people up of Elijah's day?
8. What will it take today?
9. Have people changed in their behaviors since Elijah's day?

Reading Assignment

Read Revelation chapters 8 and 9.

Chapter 36
Study Questions

1. What did Elijah's first prophecy bring?
2. For how long?
3. Who was held accountable for Israel's descent into idol worship?
4. Why did Ahab hate Elijah?
5. Why did he blame Elijah for the drought?
6. Why was Mount Carmel selected for the confrontation?

Reading Assignment

Read Revelation chapters 10 and 11.

Chapter 37
Study Questions

1. What is the end-time church called in Revelation?
2. What was the "show" the Israelites wanted to see?

3. How did the people act?
4. How would people act today in the same situation?
5. Why did Elijah run so far away?
6. Why did he run in fear after so great a victory?
7. How did Elijah outrun Ahab's chariot?
8. Do you see evidence of the Laodicean church today?
9. Should we ever back down from what YHWH has called us to do?
10. Why or why not?

Reading Assignment

Read 1 Kings 18:20-46.
Read Revelation 3.

Chapter 38
Study Questions

1. When will Elijah return?
2. What happens when we fast and pray?
3. What does YHWH's "fire" do?
4. How should we prepare for the "fire?"
5. What is happening in the spirit realm right now?
6. How is our culture like the culture of Elijah's day?
7. What major error did the Philistines make?
8. How is the showdown on Mount Mizpeh like the showdown on Mount Carmel?
9. What did YHWH do to His enemies?
10. What did the Israelites do just before YHWH "thundered?"
11. What does "thundered" mean?

Reading Assignment

Read 1 Samuel chapters 6 and 7.

Chapter 39
Study Questions

1. Who were some of YHWH's Old Testament deliverers?
2. What are some similar things about each one?
3. What are some different things about each one?

214 Bree M. Keyton

4. What is a valuable lesson that Moses learned? How does this help you?
5. What is a valuable lesson Joseph learned? How does this help you?
6. Esther?
7. John the Baptist?
8. Yahshua?
9. What is the forerunner spirit?
10. Who had this spirit?

Reading Assignment

Read Revelation chapters 12, 13, 14.

Chapter 40
Study Questions

1. What are some things Revelation 2:20-26 says about Jezebel?
2. What do we receive if we are faithful unto death?
3. How do we overcome the accuser?
4. How do people become slaves to fear?
5. How does this translate into their lives? What are the manifestations?
6. What does "subject" mean in Hebrews 2?
7. Have you ever been a fearful person?
8. Were either of your parents or your relatives fearful?
9. What are some steps you can take to break off and resist fear?

Reading Assignment

Read Revelation chapters 15, 16, 17, 18.

Chapter 41
Study Questions

1. How are the Hosea scriptures relevant to this chapter of the book?
2. Why did YHWH have Hosea name his sons these particular names?
3. What kind of wife did Hosea have?
4. Why did YHWH tell Hosea to take Gomer as a wife?
5. What happened to her, ultimately?

6. How is this like Jesus' bride today?
7. What does it mean to state that Hosea and Gomer are a type and shadow of Jesus and His bride?
8. What are the symbols of revival depicted in Hosea?
9. How do we "sow" to the heavens?
10. How does YHWH sow to the earth?

Reading Assignments

Read the entire book of Hosea.

Chapter 42
Study Questions

1. What kind of city was ancient Laodicea?
2. Why is the end-time church called the Laodicean church?
3. What did the Laodiceans say about themselves?
4. What does the modern church say about herself?
5. Do you know any lukewarm Christians?
6. Search your heart honestly. Are you a lukewarm Christian?
7. Is your church lukewarm?
8. What can *you do* to make it different?
9. Who is the bride?
10. What will the victorious bride wear?
11. Where will she abide?

Reading Assignment

Read Revelation chapters 19, 20, 21, 22.

ABOUT THE AUTHOR

Bree invites you to share in her vision to win millions of souls for our Savior. Her mandates are: Preaching the Gospel; Setting Captives Free; Taking Back the Land; Leading Warfare Walk Teams; Reaching the World through TV, Radio, Books, Outreaches & Conferences; Youth Explosions; Staking & Praying for the Nations; Prophecy to the Nations; Extreme Spiritual Warfare; Pulling Down Spiritual Strongholds. Bree moves in an apostolic-prophetic anointing as she leads missionary outreaches and warfare walk teams throughout the USA and around the world.

Dr. Bree Keyton began her professional career as a warm-up act for rock stars and had her own nightclub act. One night, while the band was playing, she was shot in the head. Through the miraculous intervention of the living God, she survived and now shares the LORD's great healing power with others.

Bree ministers in power evangelism, brandishing a sword of steel while exercising the sword of the Spirit. Hundreds of thousands have been saved, delivered and received physical and emotional healing by the awesome power of God through her ministry.

Bree is the author of several books, an anointed psalmist, and recording artist. Her musical CD received nationwide airplay for three years, and she travels around the world preaching the gospel. She has been in twenty countries and five continents. Bree has a zeal for soul winning, healing the sick and setting the captives free. She has hosted a national TV talk show and served as a worship leader.

Bree has appeared on "The 700 Club," TBN, ABC, NBC, CBS, the National Right to Life Convention, the International Counter-Cult Conference, the National Full Gospel Business Men's Convention, the International Prophecy Conference in Tampa, the Atlanta Prophecy Conference, and the international TV program "It's Supernatural" with Sid Roth.

Bree has ministered in arenas, churches, music halls, prisons, malls, parks, high schools, colleges, retreats, crusades, seminars, conferences, conventions, coffee houses, and outdoor festivals.

Bree holds doctorates in Theology, and in Administration and Education, and is a professor at Faith Bible College where she designs curriculum, and serves on the board as Director of Research.

BREE KEYTON MINISTRIES
PO Box 17802
Kansas City, Missouri 64134
(an affiliate of Worshipping Warriors Fellowship)
www.breekeytonministries.com